HELPING STUDENTS DEVELOP INVESTIGATIVE, PROBLEM SOLVING, AND THINKING SKILLS IN A COOPERATIVE SETTING

HELPING STUDENTS DEVELOP INVESTIGATIVE, PROBLEM SOLVING, AND THINKING SKILLS IN A COOPERATIVE SETTING

A Handbook for Teachers, Administrators and Curriculum Workers

By

JOHN R. VERDUIN, JR.

CHARLES C THOMAS • PUBLISHER
Springfield • Illinois • U.S.A.

Published and Distributed Throughout the World by

CHARLES C THOMAS • PUBLISHER
2600 South First Street
Springfield, Illinois 62794-9265

This book is protected by copyright. No part of
it may be reproduced in any manner without
written permission from the publisher.

© *1996 by* CHARLES C THOMAS • PUBLISHER

ISBN 0-398-06603-5 (cloth)
ISBN 0-398-06604-3 (paper)

Library of Congress Catalog Card Number: 96-3985

With **THOMAS BOOKS** *careful attention is given to all details of manufacturing and design. It is the Publisher's desire to present books that are satisfactory as to their physical qualities and artistic possibilities and appropriate for their particular use.* THOMAS BOOKS *will be true to those laws of quality that assure a good name and good will.*

Printed in the United States of America
SC-R-3

Library of Congress Cataloging-in-Publication Data

Verduin, John R.
   Helping students develop investigative, problem solving, and thinking skills in a cooperative setting : a handbook for teachers, administrators, and curriculum workers / by John R. Verduin, Jr.
     p.   cm
   "This handbook is an outgrowth of another previously published handbook, Handbook for differential education of the gifted" — CIP galley.
   Includes bibliographical references (p.) and index.
   ISBN 0-398-06603-5
     1. Gifted children—Education—United States—Curricula—Handbooks, manuals, etc. 2. Group work in education—United States—Handbooks, manuals, etc. 3. Critical thinking—Study and teaching—United States—Handbooks, manuals, etc. 4. Group problem solving—United States—Handbooks, manuals, etc. 5. Group work in education—United States—Handbooks, manuals, etc. 6. Curriculum enrichment—United States—Handbooks, manuals, etc. I. Jellen, Hans G. Handbook for differential education of the gifted.
II. Title.
LC3993.9.V47   1996
371.95'3—dc20   96-3985
                                                                                  CIP

PREFACE

This handbook is the outgrowth of another previously published handbook, *Handbook for Differential Education of the Gifted: A Taxonomy of 32 Key Concepts* (Southern Illinois University Press, 1986) that I wrote with the late Dr. Hans G. Jellen. Our intention after that was to continue on and develop another handbook focusing on implementation strategies to incorporate some of the concepts and constructs advanced in the original one. Some writing had occurred, but the early loss of Dr. Jellen brought the project to a halt.

The second handbook was to be geared to the highly gifted student and not the general population. However, after considerable thinking I decided to gear it to all students and *help these young people develop skills in cooperative investigation, problem solving, and critical thinking and to produce new knowledge for themselves (true knowledge production)*. I feel that all students should have the opportunity to pursue this problem solving process in their schooling and make learning a more meaningful experience. I feel that the qualities developed in both the cognitive and affective domains, and the psychomotor when appropriate, resulting from a cooperative team investigative approach should be shared with as many students as possible. All should have the opportunity to explore new and unknown areas, develop investigative skills, and learn to work together in their schooling.

Although much of the emphasis in this handbook will be placed on developing investigative, problem-solving and thinking skills, I still recognize and advocate the importance of students working together in a cooperative and democratic setting solving problems that are meaningful to them. Earlier, in my first major publication (*Cooperative Curriculum Improvement*, Prentice-Hall, 1967), I advocated that teachers and administrators work together in a democratic, cooperative team setting to solve their curricular problems in their schools. Now it is time for students to do the same thing. The benefits are numerous.

Cooperative learning, as we all know, is an instructional tool just like a lecture, demonstration, one-on-one instruction and other forms. It cannot and should not be used all the time as an instructional mode. But, cooperative learning coupled with scientific investigation is one that all students should encounter during their education opportunities in class. It can be used in the elementary school, in the middle school with its extended time periods, in the high school for major term projects in selected classes, and at the post-secondary level again for major class projects in a variety of areas. Students must have this learning experience in their education programming.

I wish to encourage social responsiveness and responsibility in the process. These two qualities were emphasized in the original gifted handbook and are very important to the development of young people in our society. I suggest that all of this can occur in a cooperative team setting under the leadership of an effective teacher/instructor.

Perhaps the key to this process, then, is the professional educator's behavior. This handbook will attempt to assist the teacher, the administrator and the curriculum worker by providing organizational ideas and instructional procedures. Further, it will offer assistance on evaluation processes, both formative and summative, and offer other guides on effective investigation of real problems.

The Handbook is divided into parts. Part I will offer a brief rationale on the team approach drawing heavily on the research and ideas associated with cooperative learning, and then on the importance of investigative processing and problem solving for new learning. It will illustrate the effectiveness of cooperative team work and the need for knowledge production as a viable alternative to knowledge consumption. The team approach, or every player having to contribute to the success of reaching a goal, and generating new knowledge are critical here.

Part II will present ideas on organizing for this process in a step-by-step approach. It offers procedures, cautions, and useful strategies for the teacher/instructor to consider. Part III will present some curricular illustrations that show what students in a cooperative team setting, under the guidance of a teacher/instructor, can accomplish as they pursue meaningful, student-initiated and student executed topics for investigation. At the end is a bibliography.

I would like to thank Norma Colyer for her assistance in the preparation of this manuscript. Her help is greatly appreciated.

I would like to dedicate this effort to my late colleague, Hans G. Jellen, a true scholar.

Finally, I would like to thank again my family, Janet, John III, Susan, Sue, and John IV. Their continued support is what keeps me going.

JRV, Jr.
Carbondale, Illinois

CONTENTS

Preface	v
Part I. A Rationale for Cooperative Team Investigation	3
Introduction	3
Cooperative Team Learning	4
Cooperative Learning Effectiveness	5
Investigation and Knowledge Production	7
The Process	8
The Teacher's/Instructor's Role	9
Part II. Planned Phases of Cooperative Team Investigation	11
I. Organizational Process Phase	11
Rationale	11
Initial Sessions	12
Establishing Focus	13
Forming Groups or Task Teams	13
Providing Leadership	13
Assessing Team Process and Leadership	14
Planning Research Projects	15
Planning the Environment for Team Investigation	16
Selected Strategy I.1 "Getting Acquainted"	17
Selected Strategy I.2 "Personal Inventories"	18
Selected Strategy I.3 "Brainstorming"	19
Selected Strategy I.4 "Interest Inventory and Ranking"	21
Selected Strategy I.5 "DOs and DON'Ts for Managing Teams"	22
Selected Strategy I.6 "DOs and DON'Ts of Leadership Development of Students"	23
Selected Strategy I.7 "Observing Leadership"	24

	Selected Strategy I.8 "Observing Team Activities"	26
	Selected Strategy I.9 "Self-Assessment"	27
	Selected Strategy I.10 "Scientific Inquiry"	28
II.	Information Processing Phase	29
	Rationale	29
	Identifying the Information Sources	29
	Prioritizing and Screening of Sources	30
	Establishing Task Specificity	30
	Managing and Coordinating Tasks	31
	Training in Information Processing	31
	Assessment of Relevant Data	31
	Selected Strategy II.1 "Creating a Speaker's Bureau"	33
	Selected Strategy II.2 "Locating Information Sources"	34
	Selected Strategy II.3 "Developing Interviewing and Surveying Skills"	35
	Selected Strategy II.4 "Contractual Agreements"	37
	Selected Strategy II.5 "Developing a Management Schedule"	38
	Selected Strategy II.6 "Eclectic Information Processing"	39
	Selected Strategy II.7 "Organizing Relevant Data"	40
	Selected Strategy II.8 "Analyzing Relevant Data"	41
III.	Implementation Phase I	43
	Rationale	43
	Defining an Approach	43
	Securing Materials	44
	Beginning and Completing Projects	44
	Selected Strategy III.1 "Project Decision-Making Procedure"	45
	Selected Strategy III.2 "Time Management Procedure"	47
	Selected Strategy III.3 "Developing a Master Contract"	48
	Selected Strategy III.4 "General Procedure for Completion of Project"	49
IV.	Evaluation Phase I	51
	Rationale	51
	Process Evaluation	51
	Product Evaluation	52
	Selected Strategy IV.1 "Process Individual Assessment"	53
	Selected Strategy IV.2 "Preliminary Team Assessment"	55

	Selected Strategy IV.3 "Evaluation of Real Objects"	57
	Selected Strategy IV.4 "Evaluation for On-Paper Research"	59
V.	Refinement and Implementation Phase II	61
	Rationale	61
	Process Refinement and Implementation	62
	Product Refinement and Implementation	62
	Selected Strategy V.1 "Individual Intervention and Restructuring"	64
	Selected Strategy V.2 "Team Intervention and Restructuring"	65
	Selected Strategy V.3 "Expert Review and Assessment"	67
VI.	Evaluation Phase II	69
	Rationale	69
	Summative Process Evaluation	69
	Summative Product Evaluation	70
	Selected Strategy VI.1 "Summative Individual Assessment"	71
	Selected Strategy VI.2 "Summative Team Assessment"	73
	Selected Strategy VI.3 "Quality of Research Project"	75
Flowchart for Overall Perspective on Cooperative Knowledge Production		78

Part III. Curricular Illustrations   79

Introduction   79
Illustration I "A School Problem"   80
    Problem Finding/Sensing   80
    Problem Analysis   81
    Problem Formulation   81
    Proposed Solution   81
    Consequences of the Proposed Solution   81
    Fact-Finding Activities   82
    Utilizing the Scientific Method   82
    Analysis of Data/Information   82
    Formulation and Refinement of a Tentative Solution 83
    Testing and Evaluating the Proposed Solution   83
    Refinement and Intervention   83
    Implementation and Summative Evaluation   84
    Performance Outcomes   84

Illustration II "A Major Health Problem" 84
    Problem Finding/Sensing 84
    Problem Analysis 85
    Problem Formulation 85
    Proposed Solutions 85
    Consequences of the Proposed Solution 86
    Fact-Finding Activities 86
    Utilizing the Scientific Method 86
    Analysis of Data/Information 87
    Formulation and Refinement of Tentative Solution 87
    Testing and Evaluating the Proposed Solution 87
    Refinement and Intervention 88
    Implementation and Summative Evaluation 88
    Presentations and Follow-Up 88
Illustration III "A History Problem" 89
    Problem Finding/Sensing 89
    Problem Analysis 89
    Problem Formulation 90
    Suggested Solutions 90
    Discussion of the Consequences 90
    Fact-Finding Missions 91
    Utilizing the Scientific Method 91
    Analysis of Data 92
    Formulation and Refinement of a Tentative Solution 92
    Testing and Evaluating the Proposed Solution 93
    Refinement and Intervention 93
    Presentation and Summative Evaluation 93

Bibliography 95
Index 99

HELPING STUDENTS DEVELOP INVESTIGATIVE, PROBLEM SOLVING, AND THINKING SKILLS IN A COOPERATIVE SETTING

PART 1

A RATIONALE FOR COOPERATIVE TEAM INVESTIGATION

Introduction

There are many demands, tasks, and mandates placed on our public schools today and there will likely be many more in the future as we move to preparing young people for the 21st century. Many of these demands and mandates cry for more math, science, technology, and computers in the curriculum which can prepare young people to become literate and functional in the new technologies and be ready to lead the world in these areas. This enhancement in the "high tech" cognitive areas is certainly needed, but are there other behaviors that will aid young people as they find their place in society and provide other kinds of leadership. Do we not need people who can cooperate, find solutions together, and participate in shared decision making? Do we not need people who are socially responsive and responsible individuals? And, do we not need people who will enhance the democratic ideal? Will these important demands be met? Jarolimek and Parker (1993) argue that "societies organized under the democratic ideal place special demands on their school systems. Children in these societies need to be educated to be the kind of citizens who can and will share in popular sovereignty" (p. 391).

Democracy demands participation and the democratic ideal extends to involvement of people in public life. Everyone is needed to solve problems in society. We need people who can work well together in task-oriented situations and bring resolution to all kinds of problems facing us; these task oriented groups are critical to our success in the future. These groups will have to learn to work together to solve problems and "their members are mutually dependent on one another for planning the work and getting it done successfully" (Jarolimek and Parker, 1993, p. 391).

Where can these behaviors be developed and practiced early on? One of the most obvious places would be in the schools. The schools through their program efforts can serve as *the* most significant place for the needed development. The school and the actual classroom are the places where young people can and must develop the appropriate attitudes and skills for cooperation and democratic participation, and they can actually serve as a laboratory, a place of apprenticeship, to successfully acquire these behaviors.

The school is not only a place of learning specific cognitive skills, but a place where significant affective behaviors can be developed. Our schools bring diverse groups of youngsters together with very different backgrounds. We are seeing more minorities in our school populations than ever before, and minorities and the majority must work together in school and later in life to foster good democratic participation in decision making and problem solving. The school can then provide a place where all can learn to appreciate others and their contributions, and build effective working relationships early on. How can we build some of these important democratic, affective behaviors and at the same time enhance the high cognitive development that is also needed? Perhaps we might explore a cooperative team model for the learning for students.

Cooperative Team Learning

What is cooperative team learning? As opposed to competitive learning or individualistic learning, it is a term "that refers to instructional methods in which students of all levels work together in small groups toward a group goal" (Slavin, 1987, p. 8); active learning teams of students work together to reach common goals. A major factor is that the success of one student helps others to be successful in the teams. Significant parts of the curriculum are organized around tasks, problems, and projects that small mixed-ability groups or teams can work through. Unlike ability grouping and teacher-centered instruction, it brings students together to attack problems that are important to them.

Cooperative team learning differs from the traditional group work used in classrooms in the past. There is a big difference between putting students into a group to learn and in developing true cooperative team learning among students. Johnson, Johnson, Holubec, and Roy (1984) suggest that there are four basic elements that must be included in team work to make it truly a cooperative endeavor. The first major element is positive interdependence where there are mutual goal development, divisions of labor, dividing up resources, assigning students differing roles, and by giving joint rewards. This means that students are mutually interdependent with other members of the team.

The second element requires face-to-face interaction among students. Interaction and verbal interchange among students promotes the interdependence that affect outcomes. The third element is individual accountability for working on the tasks and materials. In doing this, each student will master the material and others can provide appropriate support to one another. The final element is that the students must use interpersonal and small-group skills which are critical to cooperative learning. These skills can be taught, and require time and methods for assessing how well a team is doing as it processes its way through a task. The team must be able to maintain effective working relationships and closely coordinate actions within it just as a football team, volleyball team, or basketball team.

In the cooperative learning setting concern is expressed about the performance of *all* students as every student will be held accountable to mastery of the material. Further, in this setting heterogeneous students with differing abilities and background should all share in the responsibility in performing leadership functions and all should share in the responsibility of each other's learning and contributions. Team members can provide assistance to others when needed. Good working relationships and social skills are of the utmost importance.

Cooperative Learning Effectiveness

One might ask how effective is the cooperative team learning approach? What does the evidence indicate as compared to more traditional methodologies? Numerous studies of this methodology appear to offer significant enough evidence to make it worthy of consideration.

In terms of achievement, Johnson, Johnson, Holubec, and Roy (1984) report, as a result of several methods of meta-analysis, results that indicate "that cooperative learning experiences tend to promote higher achievement than do competitive and individualistic learning experiences. These results hold for all age levels, for all subject areas, and for tasks involving concept attainment, verbal problem solving, categorization, spatial problem solving, retention and memory, motor performance, and guessing-judging-predicting" (p. 15). Further, Johnson and Johnson (1983) report that this strategy promotes the use of higher reasoning strategies and greater critical thinking competencies more than is found in the traditional strategies. Finally, Doise and Mugny's (1984) research supports their contentions that social interaction does lead to more advanced cognitive development. These findings should have significant meaning to those concerned about the cognitive domain.

There are other positive attributes that are derived from the cooperative team learning mode. Johnson and Johnson (1983) report that these cooperative learning experiences promote positive attitudes toward both the subject matter under study and the instructional experience itself. Students possess more continuing motivation to learn more about the subject matter being studied. These researchers further report that students working together using this learning mode master collaborative competencies at a higher level than do students studying competitively or individually. This evidence should provide some support for the carry-over of the competencies needed later in life. Further, in terms of psychological health these researchers indicate that cooperativeness is positively related to emotional maturity, well-adjusted social relations, strong personal identity, and a basic trust in and optimism about people. Finally, higher levels of self-esteem, greater acceptance and support by others, and greater expectations toward more rewarding and enjoyable future interaction with peers result from the cooperative team mode. Again, some more much-needed qualities for future living are derived from this learning process.

In terms of team composition Slavin (1987) suggests that most cooperative team learning methods work equally for all types of students. "While occasional studies find particular advantages for high or low achievers, boys or girls, and so on, the great majority find equal benefits for all types of students. Sometimes a concern is expressed that cooperative learning will hold back high achievers. The research provides absolutely no support for this claim; high achievers gain from cooperative learning" (p. 20).

Therefore, with this mode of classroom operation there appear to be many results that are desirable for the growth of students, all students. With this degree of success derived from cooperative team learning in mind, we now turn to learning new things or generating new knowledge on the part of students or what might be considered as knowledge production.

Investigation and Knowledge Production

Within the domain of cooperative team investigation there must be opportunities to examine various issues, define goals, and proceed to generate new knowledge on the part of the learners; the learners should become responsible knowledge producers. "Knowledge producers are those who produce and evaluate new knowledge from existing knowledge and therefore differ from the traditional 'knowledge utilizers'" (Jellen and Verduin, 1986, p. 6). This effort is a departure from the factual knowledge consumption and regurgitation that is quite predominant in normal schooling today; it is a shift from fact-giving to fact-finding. This socially-responsible knowledge production is a demand for weighing the consequences in personal, social and environmental terms before the implementation of new knowledge takes place. The outcome of knowledge production in students "is a mental restructuring of values, attitudes, and beliefs toward more altruistic, cooperative, and responsive-responsible behaviors" (Jellen and Verduin, 1986, p. 7).

With sound cooperative, investigative team learning the emphasis should be placed on learning how to learn, to question, to apply, to explore, and to produce new ideas, concepts, and hypotheses. Using this approach has the potential to reinforce problem solving, to pursue a wide range of interests, to discover new ways of doing things, and to enjoy learning through student-designed simulations and/or projects. With effective cooperative thinking, exploration and investigation come shared knowledge production on the part of the students. And, at the same time the cooperative interaction enhances the idea of procedural democracy as a means to display socially responsible behavior in and out of school. The entire school community can become a place of experimentation, exploration, and innovation as students pursue cooperatively problems in a responsive and responsible manner.

Perhaps the most important quality of generating new knowledge is that it demands higher-order thinking that goes beyond factual consumption, memorization, and regurgitation frequently encountered in our regular schools not only on the elementary and secondary levels but also in higher education. Terminal knowledge or knowledge utilization operates at lower conceptual levels encouraging learners to depend on memory and authority rather than judgment and inference. Further, it triggers lower-ordered thinking by reinforcing irrational, unproductive, noncritical, and shallow models of thought. All of this is antithetical to knowledge production which requires higher-order thinking found in judgment, insight, inference, and imagination.

The generative knowledge process, on the other hand, has the potential to move the teacher and student alike from concrete-terminal thinking to more abstract-generative thinking. It becomes a deliberate effort of all parties involved in the educational and developmental process of the teams to avoid mere instruction in "useful" types of knowledge with the regurgitation of "right" answers by encouraging self-motivated questioning and learning of all types of knowledge with a quest for the unknown. The shift from fact-giving to fact-finding must be the curricular basis of the program, again focusing on generating new knowledge, thus supplementing and not necessarily supplanting regular schooling.

Finally, this team investigative process is needed in school programs because it contributes to personal, social, and academic development of the students and teachers. It discourages subject-specific learning and encourages interdisciplinary thinking. And it has the generative value of forcing teachers and learners into new types of knowledge usually not covered in regular schools. All of this, of course, requires different curriculum planning and design and it requires a different set of behaviors on the part of the leader in the classroom, the teacher/instructor. The teacher/instructor doesn't give knowledge, but assists and guides students to new knowledge domains.

The Process

Cooperative team investigative process begins when students in a given setting review their general social and physical environment and come across a concern, an issue, a problem, a conflict, and/or a change. This might be termed an "asynchronous change" which causes a conflict in the minds of the student; there is a problem confronting the students, not the teacher or the existing curriculum. This "problem" could be of any nature and form, but it does elicit interest on the part of the student(s).

From the problem comes the investigative and thinking activity. The cooperative team approach moves on from there to problem definition, investigation, utilizing the scientific method, to some sort of resolution by the students. The entire process involves student-initiated and student executed curriculum activities. The teacher/instructor is the facilitator and guides the activity throughout.

The research project itself can be varied and can include a "paper" project (i.e., researching school policies), a "real" project (i.e., building a better mousetrap), and/or a combination of both. It will more than likely be interdisciplinary in nature because real problems draw upon many disciplines. It could involve ethics, esthetics, history, philosophy and/or personal and social issues. It could end up to be quite an unusual problem resolution as will be noted in Part III, and it doesn't have to be devoted to typical subject matter areas. It does, however, have to have meaning to the students as they pursue socially responsive and responsible problem areas.

It can be fun, pleasant, and action-oriented as it explores the unknown. It can, and perhaps should, be mentally rigorous as the students pursue real problems. And, it utilizes scientific inquiry and cooperative, democratic procedures in the process.

Since the research project may be interdisciplinary in nature, it could likely involve outside experts to guide and assist the effort. Many teachers/instructors are not versed in all disciplines so the need for an outside specialist may be required.

The cooperative team process of scientific investigation can be utilized at various levels of education. Elementary, secondary, as well as higher education students should be given the opportunity to identify problems and bring them to some resolution. It can and has worked well in the early grades, in the middle school, high school, and in college. All students deserve the chance to utilize scientific inquiry, think, analyze, and wrestle with significant problems. This is where true learning and useful lifetime skills can be developed in a cooperative setting.

The Teacher's/Instructor's Role

It is probably obvious that different teacher/instructor behaviors are required in the classroom than the more common ones in order to enhance this investigative methodology on the parts of students. The teacher's role, as mentioned above, is different in the cooperative setting in that he/she does little direct didactic teaching *per se,* such as giving information and facts to the students. However, much like coaching an athletic team he/she on a number of occasions will provide some instruction on selected skill development, team work, processing techniques, and leadership development as will be noted later. This kind of instruction is done to make the teams more effective in their investigative activity, and does not give answers to research work. Further, the teacher structures the environment for the team to learn the process skills and helps students assess how effectively the team work is going. The teacher also observes the team in action, analyzes the problems that may occur, offers comments, and provides constructive feedback to the team on how well they are managing the tasks at hand. These observation and intervention behaviors are critical to cooperative team learning. The teacher's role, therefore, is not passive, but an active one in teaching selected skills, in assisting in organizing, in securing materials when necessary, in guiding team activity, in identifying road blocks, in evaluating all aspects of the educational process, and in providing an atmosphere that is conducive to true investigative work. These areas are addressed throughout the handbook.

Part II of this handbook will describe the various phases involved in the knowledge production process and will offer a rationale for the phases, appropriate steps, some cautions involved, and some selected strategies that the instructor/teacher may use in moving the process along. The teacher/instructor is, of course, the facilitator, the evaluator, the intervener, the person who keeps the process going. Professional discretion is needed and encouraged throughout the entire process.

Because of the potential values derived by using this methodology in the classroom, it would appear that students should have the opportunity to participate in it. Direct, didactic teaching, individual instruction, and other teaching/learning activities are, of course, needed in the total curriculum, but it would seem that some time should be spent in the cooperative team approach to true knowledge production in the curriculum as well.

PART II

PLANNED PHASES OF COOPERATIVE TEAM INVESTIGATION

There are a number of planned phases in the cooperative team approach to generating new knowledge starting from the very basic one of organizing the students and getting them ready for cooperative group work to having the students finalize the project and possibly share in the findings of the investigation. This part will explore the six major phases and associated subphases and offer explanations, guides, activities, evaluation measures, and some "cautions" that arise in utilizing this kind of methodology with students. It will be noted throughout that the use of an outside expert/mentor is encouraged to assist both teacher/instructor and the students in their work. This is done because all teachers/instructors cannot be expected to have expertise in all areas of knowledge.

In the presentations of the phases a brief rationale or overview will occur first and then the discussion moves to ideas for implementation. Finally, selected strategies are found at the end of each major phase. It is hoped that these strategies will assist the teacher/instructor, if necessary, in the implementation activity. These may be used, or modified, as deemed appropriate to insure success. The first phase is termed the Organizational Process Phase.

I. Organizational Process Phase

Rationale

This phase moves the students from uncertainty or confusion to the identification, clarification, and resolution of significant problems. At the outset, a conglomerate of students with varying backgrounds and different ideas, experiences, and skills come together. This diverse, heterogeneous group needs to get to know one another first. Most potential team members will experience difficulty and frustration at the outset because of their diversity, and this is not unusual at the beginning of any team or group work.

Through ice-breakers, getting acquainted, and brainstorming activities, all team members can begin to know others by developing some appreciation and respect for the ideas of others. Getting to know others' strengths and weaknesses is a significant first step in the process of team problem solving. Even in the early stages of cooperation, the team may discover potential problems and develop possible solutions, which is not really bad. The team leadership may be defined or it may emerge from within the team depending on tasks and relationships. Also, courses of action should be discussed and defined. The cooperative team should become a unified decision-making body that utilizes the collective abilities of all students involved in this first phase.

Heterogeneity is encouraged since diverse ideas can be brought to the forefront and better solutions might emerge. Diversity of needs, values, interests, goals, and attitudes contribute to a healthy learning climate for the students. Team size, however, must remain flexible. The teams should be small enough to achieve functional participation by all, yet large enough to create a true think-tank and marketplace of ideas. A rule of thumb might be five to ten students per team. The team leadership must follow democratic procedures with frequent team evaluations leading to changes in leadership as situations and circumstances change.

Initial Sessions

"Getting to know each other" is an early subphase that encourages students to come together voluntarily and begin some associations. However, this is more than a social gathering for the students. It is an opportunity to stir curiosity and to develop motivation for the research to be done during the project. It is also the time to start thinking about relevant problems or issues that may deserve further discussion and possible investigation. When a diverse group of students links relevant problems with possible solutions, the stage for knowledge production has been set. The application of their collective intelligence, however, requires a team orientation towards cooperation and democratic procedures. Getting acquainted, reviewing personal ideas and looking at ideas of relevance are useful strategies here.

Caution must be established here in the fact that teachers may wish to rush through these preparatory strategies in order to get more quickly to the actual problem solving. But, team familiarity, cohesiveness, and collaboration are seen as absolute prerequisites to the second subphase.

Establishing Focus

After the initial getting to know each other, some issues or problems may have emerged which then must be clarified and clearly stated for possible investigation. This subphase of "establishing focus" is important and until some agreement on possible research is reached, questions should deal with the consideration of consequences if different solutions are implemented. Some useful strategies here would be brain-storming on relevant problem-finding and possible solutions. Discussing the consequences of the possible solutions is also important.

Since many students enjoy talking and hearing themselves elaborate on interesting topics, a concern may arise. In order to achieve early focus and to eliminate "excessive chatting," a relevant problem area must be identified and discussed before moving to the third subphase.

Forming Groups or Task Teams

Once several issues or problems have been identified by the students, clusters of interest may emerge. Students should utilize an interest inventory in order to determine what they might want to study in their exploratory work. Students should also rank their interests, adding significance and relevance to possible student investigations. Through sharing and discussion, students begin forming common interest groups that may further elaborate on potential problems, projects, and solutions. This is where the cooperative task teams are formed.

To accomplish this subphase interest inventories may be used, the ranking of interests may be done, and some combining of interests into interest clusters may be established. These strategies should lead to some task teams and problem solving activities.

The various strategies are designed to reach early consensus on possible research projects to be undertaken. Without utilization of these effective devices, the discussions might draw on for weeks without ever reaching an agreement. Teachers must be aware of this.

Providing Leadership

After the formation of working teams, student leaders are identified, the next subphase. If necessary, leadership could be provided initially by the teacher, but it should eventually emerge from the task team itself. Initial leadership tasks might involve reporting to the entire class on progress, assigning some tasks to team members, and running some activities that facilitate cooperative work. Leadership of working teams should also be democratic in nature and should change as different tasks confront the task teams. All team members should experience leadership responsibilities from time to time. With the systematic development of team work and student leadership, some additional discussion and clarification of problem areas might occur.

Teachers should not push in order to get a leader for a certain task to be accomplished. The leadership along with the teacher should facilitate team discussion instead of the task at hand, and then ask for volunteers to get the job done. Some tasks, however, find more volunteers than others, and, therefore, it is important to keep a balance between "chiefs and Indians."

Assessing Team Process and Leadership

The next subphase is that of assessing the team process and leadership and requires a periodic check of progress to see that the students are not spinning their wheels and becoming nonproductive. Although frustration and false starts are not unusual in cooperative team work, some corrective measures may need to be instituted to insure that cooperative processes and appropriate decisions regarding direction and mission are being accomplished. Information needs to be gathered to determine if the team is functioning well and if the leadership is effective. If progress has stalled, process evaluation of the students should be utilized to identify shortcomings. Changes in leadership may be necessary, and other adjustments may alleviate problems related to the team work. The problem may be a personality clash, rather small in nature and easily resolved by rotating team membership. In any case, the teacher must continuously assess the cooperative team process and leadership style so that interest and motivation remain high. The teacher may use some group observation scale and self-assessment instruments as a strategy to determine the processing so far.

Since personality clashes do and will occur and other problems in team processing are possible, the teacher must intervene and be prepared to confront the various task teams and their respective leadership by explaining and rationalizing the rotation or exchange of team members as well as team leadership.

Planning Research Projects

Once a specific problem is identified, and task teams as well as leadership have been established, the students should begin to plan a research project intended to bring some resolution to the problems discussed previously. Since it is the sole aim of all planned research to discover and to produce knowledge, a well-organized research project should facilitate knowledge production on the parts of the students and their teacher. Planned research becomes, therefore, a demand for the application of the "scientific method" as a means to gain insight into undiscovered truths.

Based on inductive reasoning, this form of logic: (1) identifies a given problem that defines the direction and potential goals of the quest; (2) gathers and classifies data with the hope of resolving the problem; (3) states a tentative hypothesis both as a logical means of locating the data and as an aid to resolving the problems; (4) tests empirically the hypothesis by processing and interpreting the data; and (5) resolves the primary question linked to original problem which initiated the research in the first place.

Additional questions need to be answered at this point: (a) Why does this type of problem need resolution? Is it important? (b) Can this problem be solved by utilizing the scientific and project methods? (c) Which academic disciplines are principally concerned with certain types of research questions as well as research problems providing factual and operative knowledge necessary for problem resolution? (d) What is the best research method for a given problem? And, Why?

Once these questions have been answered, some specific goals can be established. Numerous strategies, activities, materials, resources, and facilities need to be identified. Finally, some measures can be listed to determine if progress is being made on the research project (i.e., formative evaluation). Many of the initial activities can be and perhaps should be, somewhat tentative in nature. As students enter into true knowledge production, new horizons and directions may emerge for them to be considered. However, systematic planning of the research format(s) and subsequent methodologies is critical at the outset in order to achieve measureable and valid results.

It is important to not restrict research questions as well as research problems to any one academic discipline. Better research emerges when the research team thinks of problems as arising out of broad, generic, and interdisciplinary areas. Nevertheless, the direction to be taken must be valid and reliable by utilizing the steps of the scientific method as a means for the search of new knowledge.

Planning the Environment for Team Investigation

The total learning atmosphere in which the students will think, discover, explore, and produce new ideas is the final subphase of the organizational process phase. Physical facilities must be such that students have the space, resources, and opportunity to pursue, in the least restrictive environment, their research activities. Further, the teacher must establish and maintain a learning climate that is positive, cooperative, encouraging, and yet demanding. In many classrooms students are frequently confronted with rigid, authoritative, and/or conformist situations which hamper innovative thought and action. The required setting for this type of team work must be progressive in nature making knowledge production its vision and mission.

The students and the teacher must assess the environment and design a strategy that assists them to overcome the problems within the entire research design that will block, stifle and/or hinder cooperative knowledge production. Without this critical assessment and intervention strategy, the proposed research project might never get off the ground.

Selected Strategy I.1

"Getting Acquainted"

Everyone is seated in a circle. The teacher asks that every other person trade seats with someone from the opposite sex and/or sit opposite him/her in the circle. Each student is then asked to provide a "cold" introduction of the individual he/she traded seats with. The objective is to develop insight, build openness, and to pay attention to detail. The person who was introduced then reacts to these "cold" observations and inferences. A follow-up team discussion should focus on the correctness and incorrectness of the observations made. A skilled teacher/facilitator might also want to address such notions as false labeling, misconceiving, and misinterpreting. Keeping the same partners, mutual interviews should be conducted. All partners then introduce each other to the entire team. Note-taking should be encouraged. On a voluntary basis, ask members to introduce all team members in a positive manner.

Selected Strategy I.2

"Personal Inventories"

The teacher draws the following box on the board including the information provided:

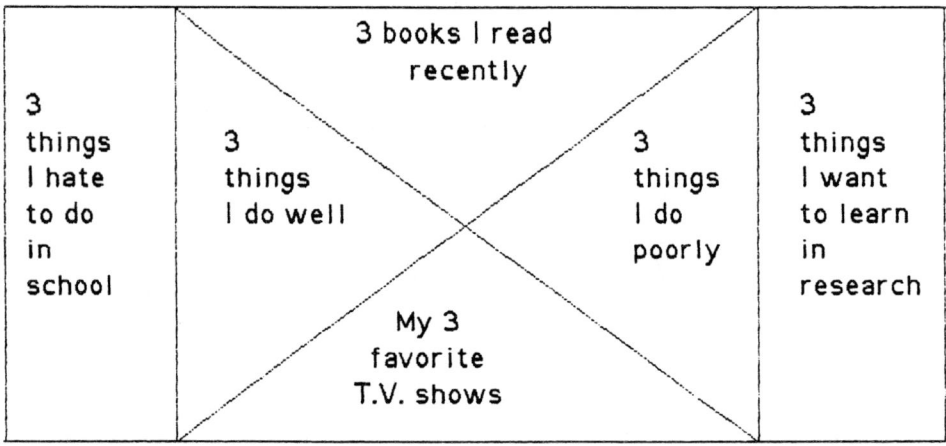

Ask all students to fill in the sections. Allow each student to elaborate on his/her findings. Let the rest of the team ask follow-up questions. The objective here is to establish commonalities of interest.

Selected Strategy I.3

"Brainstorming"

Brainstorming is a very useful group process which generates ideas. Each brainstorming session should have: A defined task; a time limit; a friendly and encouraging atmosphere where no negative judgments nor evaluation are allowed; and a fast pace.

The rules for brainstorming are as follows: All ideas are good and welcome; quantity of all types of ideas is the goal of a brainstorming session; associational thinking (i.e., adding and combining ideas) should be encouraged; and recording of all ideas must take place.

The DOs and DON'Ts during a brainstorming session are:

DOs:	DON'Ts
Cooperating; praising; respecting; listening, considering the most unconventional ideas; communicating; encouraging; timing; and recording.	Bickering, squabbling, no goal direction; disorder; silliness; loss of temper; joking; sarcasm; apathy; disorganization; and/or negative comments/judgments.

Brainstorming on issues is an opportunity to identify problems that arise in the student's life. It can deal with conflicts or changes that occur and cause some concern with the student(s). They can be in a variety of areas and must be relevant to those in the team.

From relevant problems come possible solutions to those problems. Possible solutions can be identified as a means to overcome conflicts and/or conflicting situations caused by some possible changes. Knowledge production can be seen as a means to overcome problems facing the students.

From problems and possible solutions comes a discussion on weighing the consequences of possible solutions in personal terms; in social terms;

and/or environmental terms. The discussion on the nature of the proposed solution(s) further identifies a means to overcome problems/conflicts. This, again, falls within the realm of knowledge production.

Selected Strategy I.4

"Interest Inventory and Ranking"

The following procedure for conducting an interest inventory is recommended: Get in a circle setting; each member in the team has paper and pencil; all members list their names; and all students complete the following statement: "I would be very interested in looking at and studying the following problems _____"; and collect their responses.

From the interest inventory would come a ranking of problems and interests that the students have defined as potential areas they might want to pursue by means of further research or project activities. Some clustering may occur in the weighing of the responses and, therefore, defining some ranked interest clusters is possible. These clusters can be put on the board for further discussion and interaction by the team members. This should be done to insure that there is real interest in pursuing a research problem in a major area of investigation. Several problem areas may be defined for investigation with several students working with these areas. Thus, task teams may begin to appear.

Selected Strategy I.5

"DOs and DON'Ts for Managing Teams"

In order to achieve high degrees of cooperation within each team and among all team members, the following DOs and DON'Ts should be kept in mind.

DOs	**DON'Ts**
Create a climate for all teams in which all members are treated equally, justly, and fairly as human beings.	Show preference toward certain teams or individuals.
Reinforce and reward supportive behaviors within and among teams.	Display disinterest, laissez-faire and/or noninvolvement.
Share important information with all members of all teams.	Withhold important information from some teams or certain team members.
Replace competitive schemes or behaviors with cooperative and assisting ones.	Reinforce team or individual competition(s).
Provide assistance whenever possible.	Become overbearing or too eager to help.

Selected Strategy I.6

"DOs and DON'Ts of Leadership Development of Students"

Teachers play an important role in training all students for the team leadership, and the behaviors of the teachers can set the stage for effective leadership on the parts of students. Some suggestions to improve classroom management in a cooperative setting follow:

DOs	**DON'Ts**
Encourage team interaction encounters, or informal sessions.	Concentrate on one instructional technique.
	Dominate discussions.
	Provide answers.
Stimulate individual/team contributions, suggestions and possible courses of action.	Avalanche the team with lists of "good" or "bad" leadership qualities.
Reinforce publicly and positively student accomplishments and initiations.	Restrict team participation.
	Favor certain individuals due to their assertiveness.
Remind individuals of agreed and contractual tasks/deadlines.	Ignore shy students.
Allow for total team input with regard to solving inefficiencies.	Criticize subgroups or individuals publicly; do it privately, if needed.
Utilize noncritical questioning.	Forget to be humorous and light.

Selected Strategy I.7

"Observing Leadership"

The development of student leadership for cooperative team work is critical for all students. The observation of the leadership provides feedback to the teacher and student leader which can, in turn, be used to improve the leadership qualities. Selected criteria for goal-directed and appropriate leadership to emerge can be defined in two basic functional areas, that of tasks and socioemotional.

In the *Task Functions* area, the following criteria may be defined:
1) Initiating: Proposing tasks or goals and defining team problems, suggesting procedures, suggesting other considerations.
2) Information and opinion-seeking: Requesting facts about the problem, seeking relevant information, asking for suggestions.
3) Information or opinion giving: Offering facts, providing relevant information, giving suggestions or ideas.
4) Clarify or elaborating: Interpreting or reflecting ideas or suggestions, clearing-up confusion, indicating alternatives.
5) Summarizing: Pulling related ideas together, restating ideas team has offered and discussed them.
6) Consensus testing: Seeing if the team is nearing a conclusion, checking with team to see how much agreement has been reached.

In the *Socioemotional Functions* area, the following criteria may be defined:
1) Encouraging: Being friendly, warm, and responsive to others; accepting others and their contributions; showing regard for others for their contributions.
2) Expressing team feelings: Sensing feeling, mood, relationships within the team; sharing feeling with others.
3) Harmonizing: Attempting to reconcile disagreements, reducing tensions, getting students to explore their differences.

4) Compromising: Offering to compromise own position, ideas or status; admitting error; helping to maintain the team.
5) Gate-keeping: Seeing that others have chance to speak, keeping the discussion a team discussion rather than an individual effort on the parts of a few.
6) Setting standards: Expressing standards that will help the team to achieve and be productive.

These above criteria can be placed in an instrument if necessary and applied to the student leaders. Again, feedback is critical.

Selected Strategy I.8

"Observing Team Activities"

The teacher is responsible for the achievement of cooperative learning in small group settings. He/she should observe all working groups, task teams, and/or discussion circles by utilizing some criteria to determine effectiveness. Once the criteria have been applied some corrective measures may need to be taken on the data collected to keep the team headed in a goal oriented manner. The teachers are encouraged to share their observational data with each team so corrective measures can be undertaken and justified. The following are some questions that may be answered regarding the participants in the team:

1) How well did they meet stated objectives?
2) Did they meet expectations of members?
3) Did they keep the session alive and interesting?
4) How well did they use media, aids and information?
5) Did they create a friendly and open atmosphere?
6) Did they summarize progress from time to time?
7) How well did they illustrate and clarify points?
8) Did they share/spread responsibility throughout the team?
9) Did they restrict contributions to those meeting team needs?
10) How well did they summarize at the close?
11) Did they evaluate their method and efficiency?

There, of course, should be room for additional comments when assessing the team and its functions. These above questions may be placed in an instrument of some sort for quick application. Again, the feedback to the team is critical and appropriate remediation should follow.

Selected Strategy I.9

"Self-Assessment"

The students and their teacher should periodically assess their academic and social contributions due to the success of cooperative team learning. A self-assessment device may be devised to help answer the following items to determine how each student is progressing:

1) I listened while others were speaking.
2) I was an interested and willing listener.
3) I understood our task(s).
4) I interjected my ideas at appropriate times.
5) I understood ideas that were different from mine.
6) I tried to stick to the task(s) of the committee.
7) I did not repeat ideas given by others.
8) I used concepts/facts accurately.
9) I helped in making decisions.
10) I am/was committee/team chairperson.

These items may be placed in an instrument with various choices of "always" down to "never" as alternative categories. If this instrument is used on several occasions, as recommended, the data may be reviewed after each application to determine growth.

Selected Strategy I.10

"Scientific Inquiry"

The scientific method is an organized and systematic accumulation of knowledge upon which to act and solve problems. It is an empirical epistemology and consists of five major steps. These major steps may be viewed briefly as follows:

1. **Problem Identification:** In this step a team identifies a given problem which needs exploration. The identification of a problem can occur through observation of the phenomena surrounding the investigators. This step gives direction as to what needs to be done in the investigation.

2. **Data Collection:** From the problem identification one gathers and classifies data pertaining to the problem and searches for some regularity and meaning to the data. The problem leads to the kinds of data required.

3. **Hypothesizing:** The data should lead the team to offer some hypotheses or "educated guesses" regarding the problem and associated data. The hypotheses should be precise because they must be tested for validity. Further, they could be stated as either one of difference or one of association.

4. **Testing the Hypothesis:** In this step the group empirically tests the hypotheses by processing and interpreting the data. Through deduction some predictions are made regarding the hypotheses and data. Only through continuous testing can the team predict some outcome and the validity of the hypotheses. At this point it can be seen if the hypotheses are either accepted or rejected.

5. **Draw Conclusions:** At this point the team, after complete testing of the hypotheses, can bring resolution to the problem and draw conclusions.

II. Information Processing Phase

Rationale

This major phase involves (1) identifying a diversity of information sources; and (2) classifying as well as screening data gained from these sources according to quality and relevance. This second phase might be called "learning how to find and to utilize relevant information" since the students themselves now become active and critical information seekers as well as information processors.

In order to understand the complexity of the issues surrounding a given problem, students start by finding a great diversity of information sources; local libraries, experts living in the area, and regional businesses are just a few important contacts that might be tapped initially. After these various information sources have been ranked, students are then asked to order materials, make calls, write letters, and/or obtain the information through a personal search. Schedules, charts, calendars, and contracts are used to manage time, tasks, and deadlines. As they progress, students receive training in the processing of data collected in a given problem area.

Finally, students are asked to classify and screen data according to problem relevance. This subphase requires hard work and cooperation, since some sort of systematic structure must emerge in the form of an outline, manual, workbook, time-line, flow-chart, and/or taxonomy. This classification and screening phase of relevant data, with an emerging systematic structure, is one of the most important learning skills and is crucial to knowledge production. These system-making skills help the students to cope, in a self-directed, systematic, and critical fashion, with the information explosion they encounter in all areas of knowledge.

Identifying the Information Sources

In this subphase, student teams begin identifying a diversity of information sources through brainstorming and learning how to use the library, media, computer, expert, and other sources. At first, the emphasis is on the quantity of sources. From quantity will come the quality needed to bring resolution to the problem(s) at hand.

Since team work and cooperative learning are reinforced in these learning settings, all teams involved must identify students with strong management skills for scheduling and keeping the team on task. It is quite easy to "get lost" in the quantity of sources identified. One of the best information sources is the expert guest speaker. Creating a "Speakers Bureau" first is seen as a very effective strategy for securing generally reliable and high-quality information. The introduction of note-taking and interviewing skills is another useful strategy here, and must receive careful attention.

Prioritizing and Screening of Sources

The next subphase focuses on determining which information sources are relevant or irrelevant. Critical analysis, review, and ranking of the information sources are performed until significant lists of information sources have been identified. Once quality sources have been identified, the students begin to screen and classify the sources in terms of economy, feasibility, and location. This process causes the students to think in terms of the availability of needed information sources, including experts, and how they may be secured.

Often expert guest speakers usually rank first, but other information sources must be secured as well. Too much reliance on one particular guest speaker causes a "subjectification" of information. The important concern is that a ranking and understanding of major information sources must be defined.

Establishing Task Specificity

Upon prioritizing and screening quality information sources, the students on the team then define the tasks necessary for obtaining all of the sources identified as quality ones. Tasks such as handling the procurement of the sources (e.g., speakers, books, films, and/or journals) are distributed among all students involved on the investigative team. Contracts and deadlines should be established for students during this activity in order to accelerate the completion of tasks and encourage mental discipline.

It must be cautioned that without insistence upon contracts and deadlines, the information gathering phase will not "get off the ground."

A positive reinforcement scheme rewarding students for the completion of tasks should also be in place; without it, the motivational level might remain low.

Managing and Coordinating Tasks

This subphase brings to bear the management, scheduling, and gathering of all pertinent information sources by the student team. This includes: Writing of letters; screening and ordering from catalogues and other sources; making phone calls; and developing a management schedule. This management schedule must reflect careful planning and coordination of all information to be utilized during the problem solving process. Learning to manage information sources is a critical skill for potential knowledge producers.

It should be noted that without a management schedule, anarchy will dominate this important subphase. A chaotic environment will greatly hinder the progress to be made in task accomplishment. Therefore, it is important to insure that a management schedule has been adopted and that it occupies a highly visible place in the classroom setting.

Training in Information Processing

Once the information sources are available, the students need training in processing the data. Such activities as note-taking, summarizing, searching for pertinent information, developing manuals and workbooks, organizing index cards, and utilizing software are critical. Students can further develop investigative techniques for problem resolution by using the computer, reviewing media sources, and interacting with outside experts in order to gain and review new knowledge and/or skills.

In order to conduct research independently, all members in each team must have sufficient skill development in this area. If not, the research project will likely fail. Frequent "remedial intervention" on the part of the teacher is essential to insure proper skill development.

Assessment of Relevant Data

Matrices and/or taxonomies bring order, meaning, focus, and economy to "information flooding." It is important to learn to classify relevant data and, in turn, to analyze them.

Classification systems are extremely helpful tools that require constant revision, readjustment, and refinement for the sake of order, meaning, focus, and economy of possible information flooding. For the frustration level to remain low, teachers might utilize the assistance of competent researchers to assist in this process.

Selected Strategy II.1

"Creating a Speakers' Bureau"

The purpose of a Speakers' Bureau is to create a talent pool of knowledgable, interesting, and dynamic presenters willing to speak, without charge, and on a voluntary basis, to the various cooperative investigating teams. The table below gives an idea of what kinds of problem and information needs might be matched with what kinds of speakers.

Problem Category	Information Needs	Possible Speaker
Neighborhood	Substance Abuse	Substance Abuse Person
Housing	Mortgages	Bank Officer
Health	AIDS	County Health Officer
Recreation	Facilities	Local Parks Director
Crime/Safety	Law Enforcement	Police Chief

This illustration of assessing information needs via guest speakers or experts should be adopted for planning purposes. Consideration, of course, must be given to securing these people to make it effective.

Selected Strategy II.2

"Locating Information Sources"

A variety of information sources are available that will assist the cooperative team in locating or contacting a maximum of information for later data collection. Those listed below are some of the more common ones that could contribute, and are listed in two categories, "general" and "individual" information sources.

General Sources	**Individual Sources**
Libraries	Librarians
Galleries	School teachers
Museums	Agents
Archives	Officers
Science centers	Business owners
Local, State, & Federal offices/agencies	Researchers
Foreign embassies or counselates	Senior citizens
Police departments	Informants
Better business bureaus	Presidents/directors
Consumer protection agencies	Human service professionals (doctors, lawyers, etc.)
Chambers of commerce	College teachers/professors
Banks	Bankers
Adult education programs	Coordinators
Local school systems	Civic/political leaders
Local/county health departments	Artists
Local transit authorities	Organizational leaders
Public transportation systems	Heads of corporations
Insurance agencies	Staffers
Service societies (e.g., Cancer Society)	Operators
Local counseling services	Secretaries
Family planning agencies	Foremen/women

Court houses and law libraries	Bartenders
Legal aid offices	Waiters
Offices of public defender(s)	Mailmen/women
Offices of American Civil Liberties Union	Foreign officials/citizens
Alcohol and Drug abuse agencies	Private citizens/neighbors

These are but a few of available sources, and, of course, the nature of the inquiry would dictate others. In locating these and other sources, two judgments might be made: Are they locally available and are they appropriate for the task at hand? These are important decisions to be made before proceeding.

Selected Strategy II.3

"Developing Interviewing and Surveying Skills"

Interviewing and surveying as data collection devices are important behaviors and should be learned prior to implementing it. Some activities that may be used with students in developing these skills are listed below.

1) Divide into small subgroups and formulate a set of relevant questions to be asked during an interview.

2) Share questions with all subgroups and rank them.

3) Compose a final list of relevant questions to be asked during the interview.

4) Develop an interview schedule that suits the interviewer as well as the interviewee.

5) Design instruments, if necessary, in order to gain additional information (e.g., questionnaires, checklists, rating scales).

6) Decide on appropriate recording device(s).

7) Identify representative sample(s) and/or interviewee(s).

8) Run field test in order to revise interview strategy and/or instrument(s) utilized.

9) Create a data-gathering matrix for the recording and classification of data obtained from the interview and/or survey.

10) Discuss and/or utilize such follow-up techniques as making a call, writing a letter of inquiry, and/or asking for a verifying statement.

Selected Strategy II.4

"Contractual Agreements"

Contractual agreements between the students and the teacher are seen as convenient means to economize and manage time wisely, and to keep the students on task. If a teacher feels the need to utilize such a strategy, the following illustration may be helpful in the process.

Contractual Agreement for Task Completion

Student(s)' Name(s): _____

Teacher(s)' Name(s): _____

Short description of Task(s) at hand: _____
_____
_____
_____

Date Contracted: _____

Date to be completed/deadline: _____

Revised deadline with reason(s) for change: _____
_____

Student(s)' Signatures   Teacher(s)' Signature

_____   _____

_____   _____

Selected Strategy II.5

"Developing a Management Schedule"

A good management schedule must reflect careful planning and coordination of all information sources to be utilized for the problem solving process at hand. The illustrative chart below attempts to reinforce sound management and coordination of information sources. This management schedule can also be viewed as a "Master Contract" to be followed by the cooperative investigative team.

Information Management Schedule

Information Source to be Utilized	Topic to be covered	Date/Time	Place	Contract/ Student Initials
1. Speaker Dr. J.D.	Research on AIDS	9/6/94 10 AM	Rm 13	TB, MJ LF
2. Film: Nova/PTV	AIDS Virus	9/8/94 10 AM	Auditorium	CC, HJ LA
3. Etc.				

Selected Strategy II.6

"Eclectic Information Processing"

The formulation and use of an information processing matrix will train and help students in extracting and maintaining relevant and important information or data in an eclectic fashion. An illustrative chart appears below.

Information Processing Matrix

Information Sources	Information Topics	Information Storage	Responsible Group Student(s)' Initials
1. Dr. J.D.	AIDS Research	Videotaping Notetaking	TB & M CA, KM, & RJ
2. Nova:	AIDS	Factual Index Cards	MA, TC, & RB
Film	Virus	Workbook	BB, LB, HJ, & CC
3. Etc.			

Selected Strategy II.7

"Organizing Relevant Data"

Matricies are handy tools that researchers utilize in order to organize and classify their data at hand. The collected data at hand can be put into a matrix for easy analysis and treatment, therefore, causing a more organized approach to the problem. An example appears below.

Relevant Data

Problem to be Investigated	Data at Hand	Proposed Solution
Change of public attitude toward AIDS and carriers of the AIDS virus.	*Facts:* Information compiled in workbook & obtained from film and speakers. *Opinions:* Interviews and tape recordings. *Guidelines:* Correspondence with and feedback from FCDC in Atlanta, GA and NYC Public School System.	Formulation of school policy that deals with AIDS

Selected Strategy II.8

"Analyzing Relevant Data"

Some classification system for analysis of relevant data is important as it sorts out the kinds of data that were obtained. Each problem area to be investigated or dealt with will demand a different classification system of relevant data. The one illustrated below shows the classification of three different kinds of data obtained: facts, opinions, and policies.

Relevant Facts	Relevant Opinions	Relevant Policies
Prioritizing index cards with factual information extracted from a film and talk given by expert guest speaker.	Screening interviews and tape recordings with the opinions held by experts and laymen alike.	Analyzing policies, guidelines, brochures, and pamphlets ordered from the FCDC and the NYC public schools.
Compiling or synthesizing the top twenty index cards in a workbook on AIDS.	Recording and prioritizing these opinions, attitudes, and/or values linked to AIDS, AIDS carriers, and emerging AIDS policy for public schools.	Extracting and compiling facts and figures
	Comparing or contrasting these findings with inferential statements highlighting their similarities and differences.	Ranking of facts and figures.
	Citing major differences between expert and	Recording of facts

| laymen opinions. | and figures into workbook on AIDS. |

Drawing and formulating conclusions to be cited in workbook on AIDS.

III. Implementation Phase I

Rationale

This major phase takes the students from the "information Processing Phase" to the proposal of a tentative solution of the problem at hand. First, the students use the data systematically obtained in defining an approach to the problem by use of the project method. Goals are set, resources are defined, and tasks are identified, leading to a definite list of project objectives. The identified objectives are used in the assignment of tasks on a contractual basis.

The subphases involve securing the necessary materials for the major project to be undertaken. This includes listing, locating, comparison shopping, and buying the materials needed for the project. Finally, the project gets under way with cooperative teamwork accomplishing the tasks identified in the contracts.

The last subphase leads to a resolution of the problems identified. In fact, it represents a tentative solution which will be tested later.

Defining an Approach

This important subphase requires the students to use the data previously collected in defining an approach to the problem resolution. During this process, clear goals are established, needed resources are identified, economic considerations weighed, and important tasks are assigned. In other words, a total structure is defined for problem resolution with appropriate contracts and deadlines. This results in a major project in which the students engage as cooperative team members.

A caution is that it is common to choose problems and solutions that are too broad, so that cost and resources needed exceed the limits. The teacher must then call for a narrower formulation of the problem and its solution(s) when this occurs.

Securing Materials

Once the systematic approach has been outlined, the process then moves to securing the required information, data, or materials for the major project. Students define, list, locate, and obtain the materials required. In order to accomplish the process in the shortest possible time, proper task assignment is very important.

Assuming that time estimates in the master and project contracts will be met, always plan for additional time due to unforeseen circumstances. Therefore, it is cautioned that one not allow too little time for your project since unexpected obstacles and events will usually cause the team to exceed a schedule that is too tight and/or too rigid.

Beginning and Completing Projects

With structure, goals, needed information or data, and materials at hand, the students begin to work on the project as a cooperative team. They define and assign tasks to be accomplished by developing and signing contracts for work completion. Taking the nature of the project into account, work toward project completion should take place as a steady and consistent pace. With certain complex projects, short visits by expert mentors are encouraged in order to keep the working teams on the right track. Once the project is completed to the satisfaction of the team members, it may either be implemented and tested directly for validity, or it may be reviewed by outside experts for validity and refinement prior to implementation. The nature of the problem and/or resolution process, involved in the project, generally dictates these final steps.

A caution is that the team should not "plow ahead" if their solution or its implementation seems fuzzy. Clarification is absolutely necessary before they proceed. The teacher should and must not attempt to provide or claim expertise he or she does not possess. Mentors, instead, should provide guidance in a specific field related to the problem/solution in question. Also, do not forget the target market/audience to whom/which the completed project is to be presented when the team is developing and implementing their solution.

Selected Strategy III.1

"Project Decision-Making Procedure"

The steps outlined below should assist the cooperative investigating team and the teacher in deciding the best way to achieve a solution to a given problem. These steps should be discussed by both teacher and team.

1. As a result of the preliminary information search and processing, what would we like to find out? What means of resolving the problem seem possible?

2. Again, generate as many alternative solutions as you can. Utilize brain-storming, and then "narrow down" or "broaden up" any alternatives that seem too complex or too simple.

3. Rank order those solutions that intuitively seem most likely to work. Discard the others for now.

4. For each possible solution, what research needs to be done? List and consider them.

5. If a particular solution were chosen, how might it be stated in terms of resources needed, cost, constraints, and time? What type of obstacles might arise during an attempt to implement this solution. List and discuss these obstacles.

6. After considering each of the most likely alternative solutions, rank them in terms of the considerations mentioned under #5.

7. Have the team discuss its top choice or alternative in detail with its teacher who must agree that the cost, amount of time, and other constraints associated with the preferred solution are, indeed, within allowable limits. The teacher may have to disallow the highest-ranked solution (or even the next highest), because it is not economically, technically, or logistically feasible, or it is simply not a logical solution to the problem to be solved. This, of course, must be discussed with the team who may wish to modify the preferred solution and try again for approval.

8. It might be, in some cases, neither the team nor the teacher can identify the best solution or find a good solution to a given problem. They may then want to discard the problem to be solved and start again

by defining a new but relevant problem area upon which to base a research project. Also, it may be appropriate to consult an expert who may be able to provide information on which a sound choice of solutions can be made, or who might want to suggest an even better solution.

9. Once a solution has been chosen, it is time to consider what tasks need to be accomplished to implement it. The first step is to separate needed resources into the people, information, and materials to achieve the task. The people are team members who will accomplish the required tasks in the investigation as they will be responsible to gather the information and secure the materials that are necessary to bring the project to a successful completion.

10. It is time now to estimate the cost, time, and availability of the various resources that will be needed to complete the research project. All members of the cooperative team should be involved in the research design, overall time management, and information retrieval. However, individual students may be responsible for selected tasks as part of the investigative team.

11. Then the team should list and rank as many relevant resources that are essential to the completion of the project. They may have to conduct some preliminary research in order to estimate cost, time, and the availability of some resources.

12. Finally, it might be kept in mind that expert mentors or speakers can be very helpful in securing useful information resource.

Selected Strategy III.2

"Time Management Procedure"

Once all forseeable logistics, resources, and/or procedures have been identified and their time, cost, and/or accessibility estimated, the team should attempt to integrate the various ways of gathering resources within a given procedure, so that the most efficient use of time is made. A time management procedure will ensure time efficiency and time economy. Some guidelines to that follow:

1. One person in each team should have the responsibility for keeping, revising, and enforcing contractual agreements and deadlines.

2. All members of the team should know the why, what, when, where, and how of each contractual agreement made with the teacher.

3. If necessary, subcontracts among team members should be introduced and reinforced. Some formal contracts may be designed and utilized specifying student(s)' names, tasks, times, methods, deadlines, and other pertinent information.

4. Team leaders must be patient and flexible. Always allow for an additional 25 percent time allotment for specific tasks for the entire project to be completed.

5. Replace an "on time mentality" with an attitude that reflects "appropriate timing" for requiring feedback, giving encouragement, and providing a critique with regard to task accomplishments and project achievements.

Continuous overview by the teacher is critical in the movement of students in a cooperative team situation in terms of time on task and task completion. Individual differences dictate that the teacher must use judgment in this area.

Selected Strategy III.3

"Developing a Master Contract"

Once the team has a rough idea of what resources need to be secured and utilized at the various stages of the proposed solution or research project, it is useful to design a Master Contract in order to keep track of the various contracts and subcontracts agreed upon by the students. Again the contract deals with the people who will secure the information and needed materials. A simple contract like the one below may suffice.

Master Contract

Name of Team or Team member	Responsibilities in Terms of			Deadlines/ Extensions
	People	Information	Materials	
1. T.C.	Dr. J.			9/27/94
2. Team #2		Film		9/28/94
3. L.D. & J.C.			Workbook	10/1/94

Selected Strategy III.4

"General Procedure for Completion of Project"

The following procedure is suggested in order to begin and complete a major research as smoothly as possible:

1. Make sure that task distribution operates in an egalitarian fashion. Some individuals or teams try to take on too many, or too few tasks; they might also ask to be given the most prestigious, visible, or nonvisible assignments as their personality and preference may dictate. Such cliqueish or competitive tendencies should be consistently discouraged as they tend to cause a climate that is counterproductive to the completion of a project.

2. If certain aspects of the solution or its implementation still appear unresolved, and the teacher is unable to suggest satisfactory modifications, the most easily accessible expert thought capable of helping out should be contacted. This person might suggest changes in research design, problem statement, master contract, or resources needed that will allow the project to move forward more easily. Selecting some outside help is a sound move since the teacher is not expected to be expert in all areas or disciplines.

3. If the problem and its resolution are not valid or testable, the outside expert or mentor may recognize this and propose another problem to be studied. It is better to start over at this point than to complete part of a project that has no chance of successful completion.

4. As resources are retrieved, the team(s) should analyze, coordinate, and synthesize data; in case of a physical project, they need to build or construct real objects.

5. Again, if necessary, outside mentors should be consulted at the beginning of the project implementation, and their recommendations on when they or other mentors should be consulted during the remainder of the project should be followed.

6. By accepting mentor review, the team(s) may avoid going far off track, perhaps rendering the research worthless or uncompletable within existing constraints. In many projects, of course, the solution, once

developed, can be implemented and tested directly for validity, and then refined without outside help.

7. The teacher plays the roles of a supervisor, coordinator, facilitator, and initiator throughout the implementing procedure. It is also the role of the teacher to give the "okay" for the project to proceed or the "no" to be stopped without the assistance of an outside mentor.

IV. Evaluation Phase I

Rationale

This phase involves two major categories of evaluation: process and product.

Process evaluation refers to the assessment of: (1) The developing quality of the individual's cognitive, affective, and/or psychomotor capabilities; (2) the quality of team work; and (3) the quality of rules and procedures utilized in the project investigation.

An assessment must be made to determine if the individual student's ability to utilize scientific methodology and participate in team work is growing. In addition, the nature of the team, its leadership and dynamics must be assessed for effectiveness. Finally, the entire research process needs to be judged by expert standards. Monitoring these vital processes for constraints, problems and/or defects provides important data for refinement of further project activities and intervention teaching.

Product evaluation, on the other hand, involves an analysis afterwards of the materials or events produced during the research process. Here the outcome is measured by its consistency with previously stated objectives or criteria. Product evaluation may be formative or summative, since the final outcome may be tested directly for validity or subject to expert standards. The nature of the research problem determines the extent of outside help required. If the proposed resolution is valid, the investigation ends. If it is invalid, then refinement is required to reach an outcome that meets the appropriate standards.

Process Evaluation

Process evaluation provides important information to the teachers in three areas: First, it offers diagnostic information on the personal growth of each individual student in the cognitive, affective, and/or psychomotor domains. Second, it reviews the quality of team work, cooperative learning, problem solving, and leadership. This review of team process provides pertinent information regarding procedural democracy and shared thinking. Finally, an assessment of the total investigative process is undertaken to determine if scientific methodology has been applied correctly in the resolution of the given research problem(s). Once evaluative data have been collected and analyzed in these three significant areas, refinements can be made to correct any identified shortcomings in the research process.

A caution here is that process evaluation is frequently underemphasized in educational settings. An obsession for final products, polished results, and/or slick performances negates this important subphase of evaluation. Careful process evaluation tries to counteract and rectify this unfortunate trend.

Product Evaluation

This subphase looks at the product or the research project itself which the students developed and proposed as a resolution to a relevant problem. This formative and summative product evaluation procedure seeks out the consistency between earlier stated objective or specified criteria and the final project or product-in-process. The final outcome may be directly tested by the students, under the guidance of the teacher, to determine the validity of the suggested resolution.

The final product may also be subjected to expert opinion before actual testing takes place. In this case, expert(s) judge the students' work according to professional standards. The expert(s) then determine if the results of the investigation are appropriate to the problem and will result in a viable solution.

Once feedback from the actual testing and/or expert(s) is derived and analyzed, the students can make adjustments and refinements in the research project to correct any deficiencies which prevent the attainment of a viable solution.

It should be kept in mind that the preevaluation of the final product or research project should highlight deficiencies. The first evaluation phase of the "product-to-be" is a demand for formative evaluation which must be conducted in a sensitive and diplomatic manner if motivation is to remain high. Destructive and/or excessive forms of criticism(s) must not be tolerated and do require the intervention on the part of the teacher.

Selected Strategy IV.1

"Process Individual Assessment"

Process evaluation should occur both during and after the research project. By observing behavior(s) early in team work, the teacher should be able to make preliminary assessments which will allow him/her to draw conclusions about individual growth in cognitive, affective, or psychomotor skills. A preliminary individual assessment form should be developed for an intervention pedagogy to be utilized in any cooperative team setting. A form like the following may be utilized and expanded as deemed appropriate.

Preliminary Individual Assessment Form

Name _____ Team _____ Date _____

Directions: Utilize the following scale

1 = High 2 = Average 3 = Low

1. *Cognitive Growth*

A. Understands and utilizes scientific methodology	1 2 3
B. Makes inferences and draws conclusions rationally	1 2 3
C. Analyzes data objectively	1 2 3
D. Formulates and defends hypotheses effectively	1 2 3

Strategies for intervention and/or restructuring:

A. _____
B. _____
C. _____
D. _____

2. *Affective Growth*

A. Controls emotions	1 2 3

B. Displays sympathy   1 2 3
   C. Displays intrinsic motivation   1 2 3
   D. Withholds judgment   1 2 3
Strategies for intervention and/or restructuring
A. _____
B. _____
C. _____
D. _____

3. *Psychomotor Growth*
   A. Displays physical coordination   1 2 3
   B. Has physical endurance   1 2 3
   C. Displays adaptive movements and fine skills   1 2 3
   D. Psychomotor skills are habitual   1 2 3
Strategies for intervention and/or restructuring:
A. _____
B. _____
C. _____
D. _____

Other criteria as deemed appropriate by the teacher(s) can be included in this kind of instrument. The critical point here is that some objective information should be gathered and assessed to determine the growth of each individual student.

Selected Strategy IV.2

"Preliminary Team Assessment"

A preliminary team assessment activity is an equally helpful way to assess growth. Here, team organization, team management, team work, and the quality of the proposed research are the key criteria that must be assessed if an effective formative evaluation process is to take place. The following form is illustrative of the kinds of data that may be obtained in a preliminary group assessment.

Preliminary Group Assessment Form

Team _____ Date _____

Directions: Utilize the following scale:

1 = High   2 = Average   3 = Low

1. *Team Organization*
    A. Team cohesion and teamwork   1 2 3
    B. Resourcefulness and imaginative planning   1 2 3
    C. Team involvement and cooperative learning   1 2 3
    D. Problem-solving and overcoming obstacles   1 2 3

2. *Team Management/Leadership*
    A. Mutual respect and cooperation   1 2 3
    B. Responsibility and responsiveness   1 2 3
    C. Functional leadership rotation and delegation of of authority   1 2 3
    D. Functional exercise of authority   1 2 3

3. *Team Work*
    A. Meeting deadlines   1 2 3

B. Fulfilling contracts	1 2 3
C. Meeting task commitments	1 2 3
D. Perfecting the research project	1 2 3

4. *Quality of Research Project*

A. Quality of content	1 2 3
B. Quality of method(s) used	1 2 3
C. Quality of imagination displayed	1 2 3
D. Quality of research incorporated	1 2 3

Other comments and considerations of group work _____

Selected Strategy IV.3

"Evaluation of Real Objects"

The evaluation of real objects may occur at four critical junctures in the project process. The level of complexity of the project should be considered by the teacher in consultation with the team in determining whether or not to skip any of the evaluation stages below.

1. Are quality, cost or specifications of components important? Is supporting documentation contradictory or otherwise questionable? If so, formative evaluation of components should be undertaken as they are obtained. Comparison shopping, for example, is just as important in research as it is in buying food at the grocery store. Individual(s) and team(s) involved in the construction of real objects should strive to get the best quality materials at the lowest cost for any project where cost is a factor. Supporting documentation should be evaluated as it is gathered by the procedure listed next.

2. Some real-object-producing projects require construction or development procedures that are difficult to learn or execute or for which no clear methods of proceeding can be found by the team. In these cases, an expert in the process of construction should be found and consulted. Using the nearest-available-mentor strategy, students should locate an appropriate mentor for assistance. Expert advice may include consulting a particular text, following a specific procedure that he/she might prescribe, and/or consulting and supervising in person. As a result of the "intuitive assessment," the expert mentor will usually be able to suggest modifications or refinements of procedure that will enable the team to proceed with the project. In some projects where the construction is a complex artistic undertaking (e.g., animated Super-8 films), continual or periodic expert evaluation and feedback may be necessary to come up with a satisfactory production.

3. After the real object has been completed, it should be directly tested by the students, who, with the help of the teacher, must decide if it is a valid solution for the problem stated earlier. In many cases, the real object will be only one part of an overall presentation whose elements

must be evaluated singly and in combination. In those projects where the expert mentor was consulted earlier, he or she should be asked to give an evaluation at this point as well, unless it is not only clear to the students but also to the teacher that no such assistance is needed. Modifications of the real object may be needed, either because it does not meet the objectives or criteria set at the beginning of the project, or so that it better fits an overall presentation designed to address a larger problem.

4. At the completion of the project, which usually will be the presentation of the culmination of the research to a particular audience, it is time for a summative evaluation of the real object produced during the entire project. The assessing criteria are the same as in #3 above. Of course, Evaluation Phase II (to be discussed later) will highlight the importance of the summative assessment scheme. If there is a formal presentation to some audience(s), these persons may be included in the evaluation process.

Selected Strategy IV.4

"Evaluation for On-Paper-Research"

Formative evaluation of on-paper research follows many of the same steps as real-object research addressed in the previous strategy. A checklist, as illustrated below, can ask questions that need to be addressed during the formative state to ensure a proper foundation for the on-paper research.

Formative Checklist

Directions: Place an (X) in appropriate column after carefully inspecting the on-paper research to see if it contains the item designated. Utilize and/or incorporate expert feedback if necessary.

Questions	Yes	No	Comments:
1. Is the central research problem clearly stated?			
2. Are the subproblems clearly stated?			
3. Does the research evidence plan have organization?			
4. Have the researchers properly stated their hypotheses?			
5. Are the hypotheses related to the principal problem or only to the subproblems of the research?			
6. Is the research methodology which has been employed clearly stated?			
7. Did the researchers interpret the data, i.e., tell what the findings mean?			
8. Are the conclusions which the researchers presented justified by the findings presented?			

9. Is there any indication whether the hypotheses were supported or rejected?

10. Is there any reference to or discussion of related literature or studies by other researchers?

Just as real-object-producing projects may be only part of the presentation or research process containing other elements, including on-paper products, so may the on-paper project include the use of instruments such as barometers in the entire data collection. Even the utilization of computers during the entire production process needs to be evaluated in order to maximize or minimize the validity of the on-paper findings. Any attempt to divide print-based from materials-based research will usually fail. Project teams must, therefore, be ready to evaluate different elements in different manners as they proceed through their project(s).

If there is a presentation to a given audience, the team, teacher, mentor, and the audience itself should have an opportunity, as well, to provide evaluative feedback in terms of effectiveness, value, and the communication of the research results presented.

V. Refinement and Implementation Phase II

Rationale

Data in the previous phase indicated growth, or the lack of it, on the part of each student. All students were evaluated as individuals and as members of cooperative teams. The data collected also provided feedback on whether the research project was a viable solution to the problem stated earlier. If the data revealed shortcomings in process or product, refinement strategies must be designed and implemented.

The nature of the process assessment, in terms of individual growth, team work, appropriate leadership, and investigative procedures, dictates the next step(s) to be taken. Remediation in the process subphase is critical to ensure that cognitive, affective, and psychomotor growth has occurred in each student. The teacher must assume a diagnostic-prescriptive role in restructuring the process, when necessary, so that behaviors and project outcomes meet professional standards as well as educational objectives.

In some cases the teacher must step in and assist directly by counseling through intervention pedagogy. This may include changing team leadership and/or exchanging team members. If deemed necessary, he/she must talk individually to students and their teams regarding problems in the process. Finally, since the evaluation results can be very disconcerting to students and teams, the teacher must offer encouragement and positive reinforcement so that students and their respective teams can move forward in their project work. In some cases the intervention of an outside expert may be needed for progressive change to take place.

Once remediation and refinement steps have been incorporated into the process phase, the students will progress in their project work with improved investigative strategies, or cooperative processes, having received positive reinforcement for their efforts.

The evaluative results of the product (i.e., the research project) may reveal minor or significant shortcomings in the work to date. These problems must be addressed and resolved. Again, in many cases, outside expert(s) should mentor these corrective measures if the project is beyond the capabilities of the teacher. The expert may even serve as a mentor in residence, if this is necessary and possible, by remaining closely linked to the project as it progresses. This is particularly important if the final product is highly technical, complex, and/or in need of considerable reconstruction.

After adjustment and refinements have been made in the product of the research project, it must be implemented and tested again. This summative testing will come under the watchful eyes of the teacher and expert mentor(s), who will work to ensure successful completion of the research project. Safety should be used as a priority in research projects and should even be the subject of a legal disclaimer whenever there appears to be anything remotely dangerous about the project. Unsafe or even moderately risky projects should be avoided due to the possibility of lawsuits.

A product of a team investigation that includes the weighing of consequences must be the "leitmotif" in these settings. At the same time, knowledge production will always require a certain level of mental risk-taking which should not be discouraged. Keeping a balance in this dichotomous situation requires sound professional judgment on the part of the teacher.

Process Refinement and Implementation

This important subphase addresses the continued development of the holistic behavior of the students both in team and in individual work. As deficiencies in the total behavior of each individual are identified (i.e., in the cognitive, affecting, and/or psychomotor domains), the teacher undertakes remedial or even clinical efforts, where necessary, with the help of outside experts.

In many cases, the teacher assumes direct diagnostic-prescriptive and restructuring roles on an individual and/or team basis whereby shortcomings are identified and new procedures are prescribed. Team work and leadership qualities, if ineffective, must be remediated. A form of intervention pedagogy is used as the teacher steps in and takes a degree of control over the team operations. One-on-one discussions with students are possible, new leaders may be suggested, and team membership may be changed.

The teacher must also be supportive and encouraging since students may be very disconcerted by failures affecting project outcomes. If the initial and preliminary products of the research project are not satisfactory, new and refined investigative techniques must emerge. Poor techniques may have resulted from inadequate research questions, hypotheses, designs, and/or recommendations about the project. Therefore, cooperative team processes must be reassessed and new designs for problem solution developed. In other words, the system must be revised in order to attain the research objectives. The use of an outside expert may be required for this effort since the problem under investigation may be quite technical in nature and beyond the expertise of the teacher. After refinement, when leadership and investigative processes have been remediated, the project proceeds. Only through additional work and testing can the amount of progress be determined.

It might be cautioned here that it takes courage, firmness, and diplomacy to implement an effective intervention pedagogy. Student accommodation, hesitancy, laxity, and abrasiveness are counterproductive to restructuring and refinement efforts of this entire process.

Product Refinement and Implementation

If the tentatively defined final project has been judged inadequate, refinement must be undertaken leading to new suggestions and designs which will fulfill the original requirements. The inadequacies could range from very minor defect to those making necessary significant restructuring of the product. The evaluation, of course, will detect these inadequacies and suggest what improvements can be made. An outside expert may be needed, since the product may be highly technical or complex in nature. The expert again may have to serve as a coinvestigator and/or mentor in residence in order to assist students in revising the work. The teacher should also, of course, closely follow the project work in order to maintain control of the total direction and to check on the process variable. Once the final product has gone through a thorough refinement process, it may again be implemented and tested to see whether it is a viable and proper solution to the original problem(s).

It should be cautioned that a fascination with the production of "slick products" products to be "shown-off" publicly deters the very mission of responsible knowledge production. This entire process is a demand for tested solutions to pressing problems and not a request for impressive displays.

Selected Strategy V.1

"Individual Intervention and Restructuring"

Upon the assessment of the individuals in the team, some intervention and restructuring may be required to bring the individual up to a higher level as each performs team investigative tasks. Much of this depends on the nature of the deficiency and the diagnosis of the teacher. However, some of the strategies below may assist the teacher in the process.

For the *Cognitive:* The student may serve as an intern to an expert to learn some of the scientific strategies in research. The student may also serve as a teacher-aide or mentor-aide for the same purpose. Careful assessment of progress is required here.

For the *Affective:* The student may serve as a peer-tutor to learn to learn to get along with fellow students. Further, discussions by the teacher in a one-on-one situation will help to develop more concern by the student. A lunch with the individual or team and discussions on the issues involved could cause the student(s) to rethink some of their feelings. The student may become a classroom mentor or assume a leadership role to learn to work with fellow students. Again, assessment of progress in the affective is necessary.

For the *Psychomotor:* The student may learn to operate a specific piece of A.V. hardware and teach others to master the same. The student may design and develop a bulletin board requiring higher level psychomotor behaviors. Further, the student may learn to operate computer hard- and software and teach others. The student may operate other fine instruments in the class and discuss the many parts with others. The careful assessment of the enhancement in this area is again important.

The nature of the intervention, again, depends on the nature of the problem identified earlier. In any case, some special intervention should be instituted to enhance the quality of performance of the individual.

Selected Strategy V.2

"Team Intervention and Restructuring"

When shortcomings have been identified in the group processing of the team, and the team is not achieving its mission, some intervention and restructuring will likely be needed. Based on the nature of the deficiency, selected strategies should be defined. Some illustrative examples appear below which might aid in the process.

1. *Restructuring for Team Organization:*
   a. Assign specific task and change team.
   b. Initiate brainstorming activities to enhance resourcefulness and imaginative planning.
   c. Conduct values clarification session highlighting the importance of team work and cooperation in the team.
   d. Give socio-gram and provide follow-up discussion according to the rankings and associations made by each team member.
2. *Restructuring for Team Management and Leadership Style:*
   a. Assign task and conduct student ranking for functional leadership to emerge.
   b. Arrange values clarification session with focus on the conceptual differences that exist between the "acting *as* authority" versus the "acting *in* authority."
   ("Acting as an authority" implies having the knowledge and skills necessary to lead a team in order to complete a task that requires teamwork and a certain amount of expertise.) ("Acting in authority" implies holding and reinforcing a position of team control.) This particular form of leadership is quite often counterproductive to teamwork and cooperation and should be discouraged.
   c. Initiate team discussion on the importance of functional and rotational leadership.
   d. Explain and discuss the mission of cooperative knowledge production as "the importance of responsible and responsive

knowledge production through this entire process via the application of collective intelligence."
3. *Restructuring the Quality of Team Work:*
   a. Discuss the importance of deadlines on contractual agreements.
   b. Conduct values clarification on "promise keeping" as an essential construct for moral and ethical behavior to take place.
   c. Highlight and reinforce the importance of the application of collective intelligence; relate this important notion to "Think Tanks" in industry and "Research Teams" in higher education both contributing to knowledge production.
   d. Review or critically analyze the feedback provided by an expert, if used, on the quality of the research project. To be more specific, ask the following question: Has or has not this particular team contributed to quality work essential to the completion of a successful research project?

After the intervention and restructuring strategies have been employed, the teacher should assess to see if improvement has occurred. If not, some recycling may be needed until satisfaction is reached.

Selected Strategy V.3

"Expert Review and Assessment"

In some cases, if the teacher is unable to do so, is not versed in the particular subject area because of lack of expertise, or desires an outside opinion on the project, it may be necessary to have a review and assessment by an outside expert. The use of an outside expert to review the final research project is an effective way to refine and to increase the quality of expected outcomes, particularly on-paper research. The following questions are illustrative of the kinds of questions that may be asked in assessing the final project.

In the area of *Weaknesses:*

1. Was there a failure to state the problem clearly?
2. Were no subproblems stated?
3. Was the research poorly planned and organized?
4. Were hypotheses not stated?
5. Was there no seeming connection between the problem being researched and the hypotheses stated?
6. Was there no research methodology indicated?
7. Were the data poorly presented?
8. Were the data merely presented with no interpretation of what data mean?
9. Do the conclusions not seem to be justified by facts presented?
10. Is there no indication of support or rejection of hypotheses?
11. Was the related literature not discussed?
12. What other problems exist? Please list.

In the area of *Strengths:*

1. Was the problem stated correctly?
2. Were subproblems stated correctly?
3. Was there good organization to the project?
4. Were hypotheses present and were they sound?
5. Are the problem and hypotheses closely related?
6. Was the methodology stated and is it sound?

7. Were the data clearly presented?
8. Were the data clearly interpreted?
9. Were the conclusions logical outcomes of the facts?
10. Was the relevant literature discussed?

Finally, the general question to be answered is: From your review of the project as a whole, what conclusions can you formulate about the research in general? From this assessment by an expert, redirection and remediation can occur and the project can move on in a new direction.

VI. Evaluation Phase II

Rationale

This overall phase focuses on assessing the value of the investigation and the quality of a given research project. This phase is summative in nature and will give the teacher useful information about the process and product. Again, both process and product must be addressed to determine the total worth of the cooperative research effort.

During process summative evaluation, the teacher focuses on individual growth again in the cognitive, affective, and psychomotor domains. Also, the quality of leadership and group work as well as investigative research techniques employed during the entire process need to be evaluated. Judgments on growth must be made in these important areas, ranging on a systematic scale from highly significant growth to no growth at all. Achieving growth in these areas is a major mission of any educational endeavor and this is no exception. Significant data must, therefore, be gathered to determine the validity of process outcomes.

For product summative evaluation, the focus shifts to the quality of the final work project. Here the teacher asks the question whether or not the proposed solution will work and whether or not high levels of quality have been attained. During the evaluation the teacher can use two systematic scales to judge the validity of the solution and the quality of the project outcome.

This cooperative team knowledge production effort must be assessed in terms of the personal and social growth achieved, and the quality of outcomes attained. Without data in these important areas, no true judgments can be made nor can any real support for the effort be expected.

Summative Process Evaluation

This subphase attempts to assess the overall growth of all students involved as individuals, leaders, team members, and scientific investigators. Although individual growth is a continuous process for students, personal data must be collected and analyzed whenever a major research project has been completed.

This summative assessment process looks at the growth in the three major domains of each individual student. Further, it checks the leadership and team process skills gained during the cooperative learning experiences. Finally, it considers the quality of the investigative skills achieved during the learning project. A systematic scale, ranging from highly significant growth to no growth, is applied to interpersonal as well as intrapersonal development.

It should be kept in mind that any instruments used in measuring process growth and their vital results should be publicized and shared with those responsible for this kind of cooperative team learning effort. This will assist in developing a good measure of acceptance for this educational methodology as others review the pertinent data.

Summative Product Evaluation

This equally important subphase assesses the validity of the proposed problem solution and the quality of the resulting research project. High validity implies high implementability. High quality, on the other hand, implies a high degree of professionalism and validity.

Again the instruments and vital results of summative evaluation should also serve a similar purpose as mentioned above. These data can help convince policy-makers and others that this cooperative team knowledge producing effort is justified as an important component of the total educational effort of all students. To let these important data collect dust is counterproductive to the progress on this important educational strategy and its practice.

Selected Strategy VI.1

"Summative Individual Assessment"

At the end of research project it is essential to assess the growth of each individual in the cooperative team effort. The big question is has there been growth in the three major domains as students moved through this cooperative investigation. The illustrative form below may serve to gather some valid information on that growth (or lack of it).

Individual Development

Name _____ Group _____ Date _____

Directions: Place an (X) in the appropriate place. Also, respond to additional comments section at the end.

1. Summative Assessment of *Cognitive Development*

1	2	3	4	5
No Growth	Below Average Growth	Average Growth	Significant Growth	Highly Significant Growth

2. Summative Assessment of *Affective Development*

1	2	3	4	5
No Growth	Below Average Growth	Average Growth	Significant Growth	Highly Significant Growth

3. Summative Assessment of *Psychomotor Development*

1	2	3	4	5
No Growth	Below Average Growth	Average Growth	Significant Growth	Highly Significant Growth

Additional Comments about:

1. _____
_____

2. _____
_____

3. _____
_____

Selected Strategy VI.2

"Summative Team Assessment"

Since the cooperative team process is so vital to this educational strategy, it is important to assess the total growth and development of the team at the end of the research project. The illustrative form below can serve to provide data on the total growth.

Team Development

Team _____ Team Leader _____ Date _____

Directions: Place an (X) in the appropriate place. Since this type of data may be helpful in designing an effective intervention pedagogy, open-ended comments at the end may be listed.

1. Summative Assessment of *Organizational Development:*

1	2	3	4	5
No Growth	Below Average Growth	Average Growth	Significant Growth	Highly Significant Growth

2. Summative Assessment of *Managerial and Leadership Development:*

1	2	3	4	5
No Growth	Below Average Growth	Average Growth	Significant Growth	Highly Significant Growth

3. Summative Assessment of *Team Development per se:*

1	2	3	4	5
No Growth	Below Average Growth	Average Growth	Significant Growth	Highly Significant Growth

Open Ended Comments about this team's development: _____
_____
_____

Selected Strategy VI.3

"Quality of Research Project"

The final summative assessment is that of the quality of the research effort or project. Several areas might be assessed and the use of an outside expert (or other qualified person(s)) is encouraged if this will add to the overall data being collected. These kinds of data in this assessment make an overall contribution to the cooperative team knowledge production process and could serve as a justification for the entire effort. The following form is an illustration of the kinds of data needed.

Summative Project Assessment

Team _____   Team Leader _____   Date _____

Directions: Place an (X) in the appropriate place. Open-ended comments at the end are encouraged. A Comparison of Teacher's and Expert's assessments can be made also.

---

1. *Assessment of the Quality of the Content in the Project*
a. Teacher's Assessment:

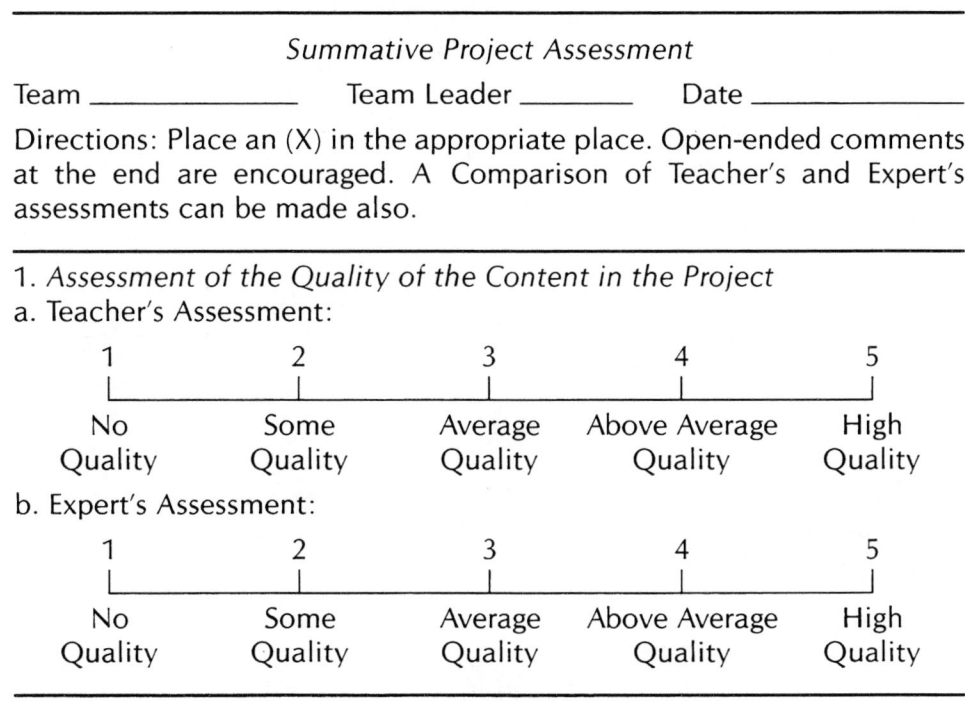

b. Expert's Assessment:

2. *Assessment of the Quality of Methodologies Utilized to Perfect the Project*

a. Teacher's Assessment:

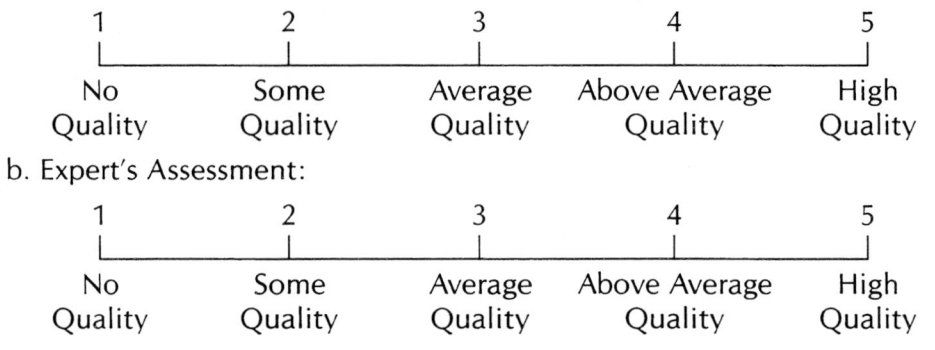

b. Expert's Assessment:

1	2	3	4	5
No Quality	Some Quality	Average Quality	Above Average Quality	High Quality

3. *Assessment of the Quality of Creativity and Imagination Displayed in the Final Project*

a. Teacher's Assessment:

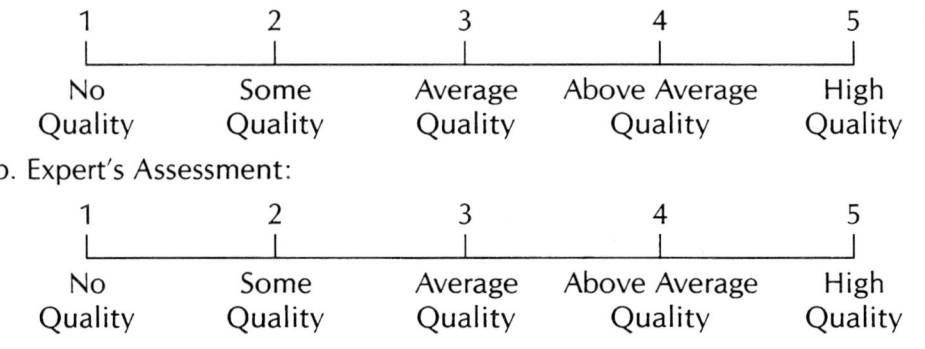

b. Expert's Assessment:

1	2	3	4	5
No Quality	Some Quality	Average Quality	Above Average Quality	High Quality

4. *Assessment of the Quality of Research Incorporated into the Final Project*

a. Teacher's Assessment:

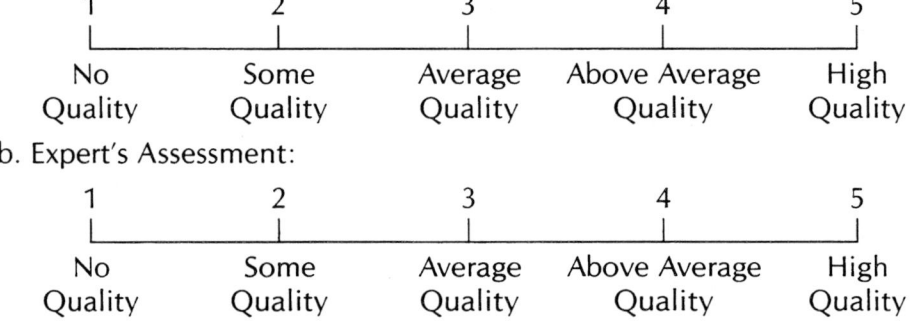

b. Expert's Assessment:

1	2	3	4	5
No Quality	Some Quality	Average Quality	Above Average Quality	High Quality

5. *Assessment of the Quality of Research Findings Apparent in the Final Project*

a. Teacher's Assessment:

```
    1            2            3          4              5
    |            |            |          |              |
   No          Some        Average   Above Average    High
 Quality     Quality      Quality     Quality       Quality
```

b. Expert's Assessment:

```
    1            2            3          4              5
    |            |            |          |              |
   No          Some        Average   Above Average    High
 Quality     Quality      Quality     Quality       Quality
```

Comments:
Comparisons by Teacher and Expert:

FLOWCHART FOR OVERALL PERSPECTIVE ON COOPERATIVE KNOWLEDGE PRODUCTION

This flowchart provides an overall view of the entire cooperative research process recommended for elementary, secondary and postsecondary levels of education.

I. ORGANIZATIONAL PROCESS
   (Initial "getting to know one another," establishing focus, forming teams, providing leadership, assessing team process and leadership, planning research projects, and planning the environment.)

II. INFORMATION PROCESSING
   (Identifying information sources, prioritizing and screening sources, establishing task specificity, managing and coordinating tasks, training in information processing, and assessing of relevant data.)

III. IMPLEMENTATION – PHASE I
   (Defining an approach, securing materials, and beginning and completing projects.)

IV. EVALUATION – PHASE I
   (Process evaluation and product evaluation.)

V. REFINEMENT AND IMPLEMENTATION – PHASE II
   (Process refinement and implementation and product refinement and implementation.)

VI. EVALUATION – PHASE II
   (Summative process evaluation and summative product evaluation.)

PART III

CURRICULAR ILLUSTRATIONS

Introduction

Part II of this workbook spelled out the pedagogical essentials necessary for cooperative team investigation leading to knowledge production which emphasizes a demand for a student-initiated and student-executed curriculum. These essentials should set the stage for high motivation, freedom to explore, application of collective intelligence to relevant problems, cooperation, and mutual trust among and between the students and their teachers/instructors. All of these phases reflect a rejection of the narrow and thought-stifling activities that may occur in regular classrooms. Meaningful curricular planning for the cooperative team knowledge production process on the elementary, secondary, and postsecondary levels must involve the teachers/instructors as facilitators of advanced learning and humanistic development rather than just transmitters of regular content.

Engaging the students in curricular planning elicits from them the feelings of self-worth, responsibility, and tolerance for the ideas of others. Team work through cooperative learning emerges, therefore, as a critical pedagogical essential for this true knowledge production activity.

Since the role of the teacher/instructor is primarily that of a facilitator in this important developmental process, he/she quickly becomes a team member confronted with tasks to be accomplished and deadlines to be met. This might be perceived by teachers as a loss of authority, and requires a different set of behaviors to effectively carry out the process. It is, indeed, a challenge to educate students for procedural democracy and cooperative team investigative activities, but it can be done. However, democratic values must be learned and practiced by all students if they are to lead in the production of socially responsible and responsive knowledge.

Part II, with its planned phases, invites students and their teacher/instructor, as partners, to become part of a think-tank engaged in research that addresses important personal, social, academic, and/or environmental problems. Part II, in other words, guides the reader through phases, subphases, and strategies necessary for socially responsible and responsive knowledge production to take place in a cooperative setting.

Part III of this handbook is only an attempt to follow-up with some curricular illustrations that synthesize meaningful content, relevant methods, and democratic evaluation. It should not and must not be interpreted as a tight curricular prescription for cooperative team work to be implemented in any educational setting. It simply provides hypothetical illustrations, formulated by a think-tank of educators, thinking about relevant problems and possible solutions that may be addressed or experimented within a cooperative setting. Of course, users of the handbook are urged to formulate their own units in a cooperative manner by utilizing the systematic steps.

These illustrations for curricular planning are offered to remind those interested in meaningful cooperative planning that all kinds of knowledge offer problems worthy of study and solution. Even though some problems might be linked initially to one particular knowledge area, most research efforts should involve an interdisciplinary database to be weighed before a possible solution is suggested for implementation. The scientific method becomes the primary research tool for the formulation of a broad database and the testing of possible solutions.

In the following illustrations the various approaches, strategies, and ideas explicated in Part II are touched on. They are not the in-depth treatments found previously, but they should give the reader some notions as to how this cooperative approach can work in very diverse areas.

Illustration I
"A School Problem"

Problem Finding/Sensing

During discussions, some students expressed individually and collectively a concern about the misuses of authority in their school. Many of the students looked at school authorities as "unworthy" of holding positions of leadership.

Problem Analysis

Since most problems are a result of conflict-causing changes, a team of these students was asked to list possible causes for conflict with school authorities. In order to keep focus during this discussion, "autocratic behavior" was defined as "dictatorial, overbearing, and capricious." During these initial discussions, students were forced to back their assertions with concrete illustrations of the causes with authorities in the school. The team listed changes that caused most of the conflicts were: (1) random changes in instruction; (2) unpredictable changes in rules and regulations; and (3) inconsistent changes in disciplinary actions taken by school authorities.

Most students agreed that whenever school authorities were confronted by pupils who questioned the randomness and unpredictability of these changes, most school authorities became defensive and autocratic, insisting upon the running of school affairs without reference to the wishes of all parties involved.

Problem Formulation

Unpredictable and inconsistent changes made by school authorities cause conflicts between students and school authority, especially since they contradict democratic values that should be taught in American schools. The problem at hand is by its very nature a socio-ethical one since it is wrong to promote autocratic values in supposedly democratic schools.

Proposed Solution

In order to create awareness of the existing problem and alternative methods in running schools, the team decided to write a didactic skit to be performed for the entire school and community, incorporating role-playing as well as role-reversals both reflecting democratic and/or autocratic values displayed (or not displayed) by school authorities.

Consequences of the Proposed Solution

In a discussion of the consequences, the team felt that in order to provide constructive criticism for school authorities and to avoid retaliatory measures by school personnel, the team would write the skit in a very sensitive manner by incorporating subtle or more indirect literary, dramatic, humorous, and symbolic means to "soften the messages to be conveyed." By using humor in order to make the audience laugh and become more receptive to the skit's message, all team members felt that school authorities might appreciate and eventually address their concerns.

Fact-Finding Activities

The team decided to develop some subgroups or task action teams to find facts and information on such topics as: (1) the psychology and the causes as well as outcomes of autocratic behavior; (2) autocratic and democratic values; and (3) literature/drama and the utilization of satire, irony, wit, punning, and/or symbolism in order to convey the didactic messages to the audience(s). All teams agreed to make use of contracts allowing them to economize time and energy or to meet deadlines. Most teams indicated an interest in contacting outside experts as a relevant information source.

Utilizing the Scientific Method

After expert input was provided, notes were shared, and generalizations made. The following hypothesis emerged: "Autocracy is based on fear of losing authority or control."

With the hypothesis in hand, the psychological expert suggested a confirmation of this hypothesis by interviewing teachers and administrators. The research questions to be asked were as follows:

a. For administrators: "Are you ever afraid of losing control or authority in your school? If so, when and why; if not so, why not?

b. For teachers: Are you ever afraid of losing control or authority in your classroom? If so, when and why; if not so, why not?

In this case most administrators and teachers were willing to provide answers to the questions. All interviews were scheduled and taped.

Analysis of Data/Information

The data collected were, indeed, informative eye-openers. Some teachers feared some students, particularly gifted ones, due to a lack of confidence in having enough knowledge or skills to "compete" with them. Others felt somewhat insecure in the knowledge of given subjects. Therefore, the teachers were defensive and feared losing control of the classroom.

The administration, on the other hand, was confronted with so many "leadership functions" that it feared not fulfilling any of them competently. Such functions as "instructional leadership" and "administrative leadership" were, quite often, antithetical to each other, contributing to a sense of losing control over teachers, students, parents, and other interest groups. An aloofness or defensive self-righteousness became quite often manifestations of fear of losing influence over any of these groups.

The groups then decided that the writing and presentation of a didactic skit, as part of knowledge production, might help others confront and overcome fears about losing control.

Formulation and Refinement of a Tentative Solution

While some subgroups had interviewed teachers and administrators, others had gathered data on literary, dramatic, and humorous means to convey didactic messages to audiences. The teams came together and then shared their findings with all. A reformulation of a tentative solution was the outcome and can be stated as follows: The writing and presenting of a short play entitled: "We Fear Most What We Understand Least."

A couple of teams got together voluntarily and began to each write a script. The best script, as perceived by the entire team, would then be presented. Again, contracts were utilized to speed up the process.

Testing and Evaluating the Proposed Solution

With two outside experts, a psychologist from a nearby university and the drama teacher from the high school, in attendance, each of the two teams read aloud its script for the proposed play. Some improvised acting out of the main characters also took place. Both experts were asked to provide constructive criticism(s) while the teacher assessed individual as well as group growth and development.

Refinement and Intervention

After the experts' rating and ranking of the two scripts with the main characters involved, all team members utilized a weighting sheet in order to choose objectively and fairly one of the scripts to be refined and implemented. The investigative team also formed new subgroups to accommodate characters and production crews necessary to get this play off the ground. Meanwhile, the teacher applied various intervention schemes to ensure total team participation, motivation, and quality of outcomes.

Implementation and Formative Evaluation

Two rehearsal performances were given, and the previously mentioned outside experts, some other teachers with their students, as well as several invited parents were asked to provide additional feedback on the quality and impact of the didactic play. Based on this important feedback, a few additional changes were made. Some students in the team formed subgroups to organize the logistics and public relations efforts for the final performance.

Performance Outcomes

The student-initiated and student-executed didactic play was presented and was judged to have contributed to a better understanding of students, administrators, and their roles in public schools. It showed how democratic values might be safe-guarded and reinforced in the schools. Frequent role-reversals, changes of characters, humorous inserts, and audience involvement led not only to a standing ovation but also to extensive coverage in the local newspaper as well as on television. The questionnaires returned by the audience were transcribed and mailed to all principals and teachers within the school system. Several schools requested a copy of the videotaped presentation in order to share it with additional audiences. Only weeks after the performance of the play, more students were asked or elected to serve as student representatives on various school committees. It was concluded that this cooperative knowledge production effort brought positive change in the personal and social ethics of the school community. Further, this unit displayed the interdisciplinary value that can be derived from a cooperative effort. Many different knowledge areas were involved in its completion.

Illustration II
"A Major Health Problem"

Problem Finding/Sensing

During some discussions, some students expressed a real concern about the illness known as Acquired Immune Deficiency Syndrome (AIDS). They wanted to get more precise information about AIDS and what might be done to cope with it worldwide. Continued discussion led to more interest and to a desire to look more carefully at this terminal illness. The team of students recognized early on that this was a controversial subject and one that could cause real conflict among people.

Problem Analysis

Since AIDS is a major problem facing all members of the world community, the students felt that it was very worthy of greater discussion and investigation. Further, it was seen as a real "conflicting issue" since some people in society would wish to deal with it while others would rather ignore it. Any changes or recommended changes in behavior to combat AIDS would stir the ire of many people, causing conflict among groups and between individuals. However, all people will have to live with others afflicted with the disease. The ability to cope and interact with AIDS patients seemed important particularly in the context of schools and school policies. Defensible policies are needed in the school, the supermarket, the church, the temple, recreation areas, and other places where people can and will meet.

Problem Formulation

After a considerable amount of debating, the team decided that there was a three-fold research problem at hand: (1) What is the exact nature of AIDS; (2) how can people live with others who carry the AIDS virus or already have the disease; and (3) what public policies should be established— particularly for schools? In other words, after a thorough search of the existing literature on AIDS, the team was to draft policy statements for their school. The policy statements were seen as a critical result of this investigation.

The complexity of this effort required the assistance of outside experts to give consideration to the nature of the problem. Along with the teacher, a doctor, counselor, and clergyman were utilized to guide the early problem review and to insure that a more comprehensive and sensitive policy would emerge.

Proposed Solutions

The development of a policy statement, resulting from a fact-finding mission that also addressed socioethical considerations for all people concerned, was seen as a worthy act of knowledge production. This policy was then to be submitted for review to the administration. A public forum for discussion and defense of this controversial policy was to be conducted by the students involved.

Consequences of the Proposed Solution

Any public policy statements regarding controversial issues are bound to have advocates and adversaries. The civil rights of the affected individual will have to be considered and weighed against the safety and welfare of the school population at large. Legal, ethical, and moral problems from such a statement could be sizeable and result in some degree of turmoil, particularly in schools with local control reflecting local values antithetical to factual knowledge surrounding AIDS. The team of students quickly recognized the explosiveness of the entire task facing them.

Fact-Finding Activities

Teams were organized to gather facts and figures on the nature of AIDS. This empirically sound data base was to be used for socioethical inferences contributing to a defensive school policy on AIDS. Such empirical methods as interviews, questionnaires, and case studies were used to arrive at a defensible body of information. Parental permission had to be obtained in order to tape doctors and AIDS patients during these interviews. Only a few patients objected to this type of investigation. The subsequent tasks, deadlines, contracts, information source identification, and information skill acquisition were defined, delegated, and carried out. The strongest and most solid input came from such outside experts as an ethicist, a medical doctor, an AIDS patient, a public health administrator, two members of the clergy, and a legal expert from a nearby law firm. A final format for the gathering of information was defined and agreed upon.

Utilizing the Scientific Method

After gathering and the classification of relevant data, additional research questions were asked in order to guide further investigations:

a. What is the incidence of AIDS in our region?
b. Are there pediatric AIDS cases in our communities?
c. What are the communicable variables involved in transmitting AIDS?

Data sources from the literature search and the expert opinions contributed to the formulation of the following hypothesis: AIDS is a terminal and communicable disease for which there is no evidence of transmission by casual contact, but for which there is no cure in the foreseeable future.

Analysis of Data/Information

Since AIDS is not transmitted by hugging, shaking hands, patting on the back, coughing, sneezing, sharing drinking glasses and eating utensils, students questioned the public fuss and fury over kids with AIDS admitted or barred from schools. On the other hand, no one has recovered from AIDS and doctors do not know how to control the virus and/or restore the immune system. There is no vaccine or preventive immunization for AIDS and no vaccine is expected in the near future.

Based on these empirical data and inferences, the team began to draft their tentative policy statement. Two copies were sent away for formative or narrative evaluation purposes: (a) The first draft was mailed to the Federal Center for Disease Control (FCDC) in Atlanta, Georgia; (b) the second one to the public school system in New York City since New York had a third of the nation's AIDS-infected children, and a city-wide policy on AIDS was already in place there. Both agencies or institutions were asked for a critical review of and feedback on this preliminary policy effort.

Formulation and Refinement of Tentative Solution

With the additional information provided by the FCDC and the New York City public school system, the policy was revised and refined. It covered the rights of students, the rules and regulations governing participation in activities under the sponsorship of the school, and disciplinary actions resulting from a violation of the policy. A rationale for the statements was appended to the policy itself. After several reviewing and refinement sessions, the team agreed that the document was finished and ready for presentation.

Testing and Evaluating the Proposed Solution

The "finished" document was reviewed by a practicing attorney, a professor of health education, and another public health expert for clarity, legality and comprehensiveness. Needless to say, there were also some flaws in the revised statements. The team grudgingly but understandably accepted the criticisms and went back to work. The teacher played a key role in this initial policy testing, giving generous support and encouragement to some discouraged students on the team.

Refinement and Intervention

After final review of the policy by outside experts, the team, under the guidance and expressed confidence of their teacher, began to draft a letter to school administrators responsible for policy formulation and implementation. After some additional polishing of the introductory letter, the team, with the agreement of their teacher, felt that the letter and "School Policy Statement For AIDS" were ready to go up the line.

Implementation and Summative Evaluation

The policy statement on AIDS was reviewed by the principal of the school. She felt that the statement was a good one and should be presented to the teachers prior to being sent to the school board for their consideration.

With the positive and written response from the administration, the team was encouraged to prepare for a presentation to the faculty and student body in a general assembly format. The members also prepared for a formal presentation to the board of education and concerned parents and/or community members. Teams were defined to prepare for these presentations and to generate some publicity for them. The local newspaper and radio station were contacted to invite reporters to the school board meeting and to the general assembly at the school. In addition, invitations were sent to parents, community members, and others to attend both sessions.

Finally, the teacher urged the team to devise an evaluation scheme in order to assess the public reactions to these presentations. This form of evaluation was to be conducted just after the presentations and would involve anyone wishing to offer constructive feedback.

Presentations and Follow-Up

Both presentations were generally well received. The board of education was impressed with the thoroughness of the work and the quality of the document. Upon the recommendation of the administration, the board passed the AIDS policy. Community members, parents, and other interested parties were surprised at what a group of students could achieve in a "nonstructured" but self-initiated learning situation leading to socially responsive and responsible knowledge production in the form of a defensible public policy dealing with a highly controversial issue.

Upon hearing of this policy statement, other schools in the area requested copies of the document for possible review or adaptation. The local newspaper and radio station gave these events positive coverage inviting readers and listeners to respond in writing to the policy-makers.

This knowledge production effort in the context of student-initiated and student-executed curricular unit resulted in data-based and defensible policy statements at providing guidance for schools confronted with increasing numbers of AIDS victims. Through a thorough and interdisciplinary investigation, the team collectively developed a statement acceptable to school authorities and community members.

Illustration III
"A History Problem"

Problem Finding/Sensing

A group of students discussing the possibility of a research project on the United States Constitution agreed that most of them considered such highly formal documents boring. They saw this attitude reflected in expressions of apathy and indifference by Americans interviewed after the Bicentennial Celebration on TV and in more recent public opinion polls. The team of students, therefore, decided to find ways to overcome this apathy and indifference by critically examining the contents of the Constitution and attitudes towards it.

Problem Analysis

The students agreed that appreciating the U. S. Constitution required a change in thinking. Television viewing had promoted a preference for fast-paced and immediately gratifying entertainment. The U. S. Constitution, however, is serious reading requiring attentive consideration of differing trains of thought for real understanding.

Many members of the team felt that their own attention span and ability to concentrate has been shortened by excessive television viewing. Few TV programs require mental effort, and viewers tend to become conditioned to shallow, peripheral, and escapist modes of thinking. Real conflict occurs when those with TV mentalities undertake mental labor instead of their customary mental entertainment through television. Most of the team felt that regular school reinforces this nonreflective attitude. In the team's opinion, the shift from modern action-oriented language to classical, formal language caused real concern and conflict when Americans tried to read the Constitution.

Problem Formulation

The central problem, in the view of the team, was that the content of the Constitution was usually communicated in ways most Americans considered boring. While the problem with the Constitution's formal language could be overcome by stating its ideas in modern language, many Americans still could not appreciate any presentation of the Constitution requiring sustained deep thinking. The team discussed the possibility of turning most Americans into deep thinkers, but soon realized this was an unrealistic goal. Was it possible, instead, to blend thought-provoking and entertaining elements in a presentation that would appeal to those with a TV mentality? The team wanted to find out by answering the following question: Can Constitutional issues be presented in a way that both entertains and truly educates most members of the general audience?

Suggested Solutions

Many solutions were suggested by the students including:

(a) A historical re-creation of the Constitutional Convention using role-playing and group encounter techniques as a means to reflect upon and to debate key Constitutional issues;
(b) A mock convention featuring famous men and women from throughout history arguing for and against Constitutional issues;
(c) A modern-day skit in which today's Constitution is debated from state or regional viewpoints, similar to the original 1787 Convention;
(d) A rap-music video version of the Bill of Rights; and/or
(e) A game in which articles or amendments of the Constitution are printed on flash cards as answers to questions.

Discussion of the Consequences

The team members did not wish to appear disrespectful of the Constitution, nor did they wish to set themselves up as privileged elite entitled to examine or change the law of the land. They agree, however, in principle it was their democratic right and responsibility to be informed via questioning. With this premise in mind, the team compared the five possible solutions. The first option had the potential to be overdone; the second suggestion appeared too entertaining; the third required acting skills which the group had to develop in a rather short period with the possibility of losing sight of the Constitutional issues; the fourth alternative was labeled as tasteless; and the last one, by itself, was considered too dull. Combining several elements from each of the options, suggested one team member, could be the most informative and challenging solution.

A mock Conventional session or series of sessions could critically examine parts of the Constitution or amendments to it. Students might represent regions, since there are far more states than students. The views expressed at the 1787 Convention would still be important bases for the Constitutional arguments to be presented. The outcome would be a thought-provoking and informative encounter to be videotaped and shared with interested parties in or outside of school. Most team members agreed that this might be the best format. It would reach a target audience of high school students, since it had the potential to relate Constitutional issues to current issues in an entertaining way, and yet promote a deeper understanding of procedural democracy by the students and audience alike.

Fact-Finding Missions

The team formed subteams to gather information. One team concentrated on the views of the original drafters of the Constitution. A political science teacher helped them find good sources such as the *Federalist* for such viewpoints. Regional and special-interest views of the Constitution in contemporary America were researched by another team. The team members were surprised by the gigantic number of books, articles, and presentations in other media, of which only a few really examined key Constitution issues. They realized that their presentation would have to be very well done in order to keep the interest of any given audience.

Utilizing the Scientific Method

The team had to be accurate in their study of historical and contemporary schools of thought on Constitutional issues. Multiple sources were used whenever possible to verify or to question so-called historical facts. Trains of reasoning used to support viewpoints on Constitutional issues were examined for internal consistency and external validity. The hypothesis to be confirmed or refuted remained the same: The Constitution can be presented in an entertaining yet educational manner to a general audience.

Analysis of Data

Analysis of data revealed to the team members some important aspects of the Constitution. The Constitution, they learned, was a compromise between divided factions that required an explicit Bill of Rights to obtain ratification. It used factionalism, through checks and balances, on the three branches of government it established, to limit the power of societal factions over the federal government. The states had practically been sovereign nations before the convention, so the Senate was created to ensure each an equal voice in one house of Congress. Private property, the most powerful interest of the participants, prevailed over the human rights of slaves. It is unlikely that the Constitution would have been ratified if it has proposed the banning of slavery. Only white, propertied males were allowed to participate in the Constitutional Convention. In other words, America then was a country very different from the nation we know today. Throughout U. S. history, factionalism, states' rights, womens' and minorities' rights, and the Bill of Rights seemed to be enduring points of contention. Numerous amendments to the Constitution have emerged from the ongoing debate.

Formulation and Refinement of a Tentative Solution

The team now expanded on the idea of a session where key Constitutional issues would be debated by regional representatives. Ground rules were established where they appeared necessary for success.

Very brief time limits were placed on the length of speeches on each issue. All members were informed about the issues that would be debated far enough in advance to permit formulation of plausible and defensible positions. Three-quarters of the members would have to agree before an article or amendment was revised, dropped, or maintained as written in their version of the Constitution. Participants also adopted the last name of an attendee of the original Convention; e.g., "Jane Washington" or "Bill Madison." Each participant was to represent the interests of the modern-day United States.

How many key issues found in the Constitution might be covered was a difficult question for the students to answer. One possibility was to cover the entire Constitution in several sessions. Another was to pick out popular or controversial articles and amendments. Yet another possibility was to focus exclusively on the relevance of new amendments.

At the end of this lengthy discussion, the team decided to start with some of the more controversial amendments found in the Bill of Rights and then decide how much of the entire Constitution the members could realistically tackle during this research project.

Testing and Evaluating the Proposed Solution

The team presented positions in class on three amendments found in the Bill of Rights. There was, however, considerable difficulty in achieving consensus on inclusion of a fourth. Therefore, the members agreed to shelve this issue for the time being. Many of them exhibited difficulty in presenting a coherent, plausible and defensible position through extemporaneous public speaking. A speech teacher who coached the school's debate team helped the team members improve their oratorical skills. It became apparent to the members that they could only focus on a few sections of the document, not the entire Constitution.

Refinement and Intervention

After some heated debates, the need for some additional ground rules became obvious. In order to avoid waffling on an issue, an article or amendment could only be changed twice by a vote of the participants. The entire section of the Constitution under debate would be voted on, aye or nay, at the end of the presentation; first by the participating students and then by the audience.

In conjunction with the teacher, the team drafted instruments by which their performances could be judged, and created questions for a "straw poll" of the audience on Constitutional issues. Reading the results for each straw poll question before the team considered the amendment seemed to be a good way to maintain audience interest.

Presentation and Summative Evaluation

The students made a two-hour presentation of key Constitutional issues before government students from a high school. The presentation was fairly well received. Although some audience members appeared bored, most of them compared this approach to Constitutional studies favorably with other presentations they had seen on TV or experienced in class. Since this presentation was videotaped, the teacher was joined in a summative evaluation by the speech teacher and the teacher who taught government at the school. Their constructive criticisms helped the students stage a better presentation for several government classes from other areas schools assembled in the school auditorium. This time the overall response was considerably more favorable and enthusiastic. This videotaped presentation was duplicated by several schools and became an integral part of government classes.

As a result of this interdisciplinary research project, the students and their audiences had gained a better understanding of the workings of the 1787 convention, and of modern-day interpretations of the Constitution. By proving that learning about the Constitution did not have to be boring, the team proved that most Americans could appreciate this document if approached in the right manner. Such increased appreciation of the Constitution is important to the survival of a procedural democracy.

BIBLIOGRAPHY

Augustine, D.K., Gruber, K.D. & Hanson, L.R. (Dec. '89/Jan. '90). "Cooperation works!" *Educational Leadership* 47(4), 4–7.

Bloom, B.S., et al. (1956). *Taxonomy of educational objectives, the classification of educational goals, handbook I; Cognitive domain.* New York: McKay.

Bossert, S.T. (1988–89). "Cooperative activities in the classroom," In E. Z. Rothkopf (ed.). *Review in Education* (vol. 15). Washington, D.C.: American Educational Research Association.

Dansereau, D.F. (1988). "Cooperative learning strategies," In E. E. Weinstein, E. T. Goetz, and P. A. Alexander (eds.). *Learning and Study Strategies: Issues in Assessment, Instruction, and Evaluation.* New York: Academic Press.

Doise, W. & Mugny, G. (1984). *The social development of the individual.* New York: Pergamon Press.

Edwards, C. & Stout, J. (Dec. '89/Jan. '90). "Cooperative learning: The first year," *Educational Leadership,* 47(4), 38–41.

Ellis, S. S. (Dec. '89/Jan. '90). "Introducing cooperative learning," *Educational Leadership,* 47(4), 34–37.

Foyle, H. C., Lyman, L., & Thies, S. A. (1993). *Cooperative learning in early childhood education.* Washington, DC: National Education Association.

Harrow, A. (1972). *A taxonomy of the psycho-motor domain.* New York: McKay.

Holmes, B. (1981). *Comparative education: Some considerations of methods.* London, U.K. Allen & Unwin.

Hoover, K.H. (1981). *A sourcebook of student activities.* Boston: Allyn & Bacon.

Isaac, S. & Michael, W. (1981). *Handbook in research and evaluation* (2nd ed.). San Diego: Edits Publishers.

Jarolimek, J., & Parker, W. C. (1993). *Social studies in elementary education* (9th ed.). New York: Macmillan.

Jellen, H. G., & Verduin, J. R., Jr. (1986). *Handbook for differential education of the gifted: A taxonomy of 32 key concepts.* Carbondale, IL: Southern Illinois University Press.

Johnson, D. W. & Johnson, R. T., Holubec, E. J. & Roy, P. (1984). *Circles of learning: Cooperation in the classroom.* Washington, DC: Association for Supervision and Curriculum Development.

Johnson, D. W. & Johnson, R. T. (1994). *Learning together and alone: Cooperative, competitive and individualistic learning.* Boston: Allyn & Bacon.

Johnson, D. W. & Johnson, R. T. (Dec. '89/Jan. '90). "Social skills for successful group work," *Educational Leadership, 47*(4), 29–33.

Johnson, D. W., & Johnson, R. T. (1983). "The socialization and achievement crisis: Are cooperative learning experiences the solution?" In L. Bickman (ed.), *Applied Social Psychology Annual 4.* Beverly Hills, CA: Sage.

Joyce, B., & Well, M. (1972). *Models of teaching.* Englewood Cliffs, NJ: Prentice-Hall.

Kagan, S. (Dec. '89/Jan. '89). "The structured approach to cooperative learning," *Educational Leadership, 47*(4), 12–15.

Krathwohl, D., et al. (1964). *Taxonomy of educational objectives, the classification of educational goals: Handbook II: The affective domain.* New York: McKay.

Leedy, P.D. (1981). *Practical research.* New York: Macmillan.

Lyman, L. & Foyle, H. C. (1993). *Cooperative grouping for interactive learning: Students, teachers, and administrators.* Washington, DC: National Education Association.

Magoon, R. & Jellen, H.G. (1980). *Capitalizing on student interests and motivation.* Poquoson, VA: Human Development Press.

Magoon, R. & Jellen, H.G. (1980). *Leadership development: Democracy in action.* Poquoson, VA: Human Development Press.

Miel, A. (1952). *Cooperative procedures in learning.* New York: Teachers College, Columbia University.

Newman, F.M. & Thompson, J. (1987). *Effects of cooperative learning on achievement in secondary schools: A summary of research.* Madison, WS: University of Wisconsin, National Center on Effective Secondary Schools.

1973 annual handbook for group facilitators. (1973) San Diego: University Associates.

Pfeiffer, J. W., et al. (1974). *A handbook of structured experiences for human relations training* (Vol. III). San Diego: University Associates.

Putnam, J. W. (ed). (1994) *Cooperative learning and strategies for inclusion: Celebrating diversity in the classroom.* Baltimore, MD: Paul H. Brookes.

Rottier, J. & Ogan, D. J. (1993). *Cooperative learning in middle-level Schools.* Washington, DC: National Education Association.

Sapon-Shevin, M. & Schniedewind, N. (Dec. '89/Jan. '90). "Selling cooperative learning without selling it short," *Educational Leadership, 47*(4), 63–65.

Schultz, J. L. (Dec. '89/Jan. '90). "Cooperative learning: Refining the Process," *Educational Leadership, 47*(4), 43–45.

Sharan, S. (1980). "Cooperative learning in small groups: Recent methods and effects on achievement, attitudes, and ethnic relations," *Review of Educational Research, 50*(2), 241–271.

Sharan, S. & Hertz-Lazarowitz, R. (1980). "A group investigation method of cooperative learning in the classroom." In S. Sharan, et al. (eds.) *Cooperation in Education.* Provo, UT: Brigham Young University Press.

Sharan, S., Hertz-Lazarowitz, R., Bejarano, Y., Raviv, S., & Sharan, Y. (1984). *Cooperative learning in the classroom: Research in desegregated schools.* Hillsdale, NJ: Erlbaum.

Sharan, S. & Lazarowitz, R. (1986). "A group-investigation method of cooperative learning in the classroom," In S. Sharan, et al. (eds.) *Cooperation in Education.* Provo, UT: Brigham Young University Press.

Sharan, S. & Sharan, Y. (1976). *Small group teaching.* Englewood Cliffs, NJ: Educational Technology.

Sharan, S. & Shaulov, Y. (1989). "Cooperative learning, motivation to learn and academic achievement." In S. Sharan (ed.), *Cooperative Learning: Theory and Research.* New York: Praeger.

Sharan, Y. & Sharan, S. (Dec. '89/Jan. '90). "Group investigation expands cooperative learning," *Educational Leadership, 47*(4), 17–21.

Simpson, E. J. (1972). "The classification of educational objectives in psychomotor domain." In F. Urbach (ed.), *The Psychomotor Domain.* Washington, D.C.: Gryphon House.

Slavin, R. E. (1988). "Cooperative learning and student achievement," *Educational Leadership, 45*(2), 31–33.

Slavin, R. E. (1989). "Cooperative learning and student achievement," In *School and Classroom Organization.* In R. E. Slavin (ed.) Hillsdale, NJ: Erlbaum.

Slavin, R. E. (1987). *Cooperative learning: Student teams* (2nd ed). Washington, DC: National Education Association.

Slavin, R. E. (Dec. '89/Jan. '90). "Research on cooperative learning: Consensus and controversy," *Educational Leadership, 47*(4), 52–54.

Slavin, R. E. (1994). *Student team learning: A practical guide to cooperative learning* (3rd ed.). Washington, DC: National Education Association.

Schmuck, R. A. (1983). *Group processes in the classroom.* Dubuque, IA: W. C. Brown.

INDEX

A

"Analyzing Relevant Data" Strategy, 41–42
Assessing Team Process and Leadership, 14
Assessment—General (*see* Evaluation)

B

Beginning and Completing Projects, 45
"Brainstorming" Strategy, 19–20

C

"Contractual Agreements" Strategy, 37
Cooperative Learning Effectiveness, 5–6
Cooperative Team Investigation, Rationale for, 3–11
Cooperative Team Learning, 4–5
Cooperative Team Process, 8–9
"Creating a Speakers Bureau" Strategy, 33
CURRICULAR ILLUSTRATION I "A SCHOOL PROBLEM", 80–84
CURRICULAR ILLUSTRATION II "A MAJOR HEALTH PROBLEM", 84–88
CURRICULAR ILLUSTRATION III "A HISTORY PROBLEM", 89–93

D

Data (*see* Information)
Defining an Implementation Approach, 43
"Developing a Management Schedule" Strategy, 38
"Developing a Master Contract" Strategy, 48
"Developing Interviewing and Surveying Skills" Strategy, 36
"DOs and DON'Ts for Managing Teams" Strategy, 22
"DOs and DON'Ts of Leadership Development of Students" Strategy, 23

E

"Eclectic Information Processing" Strategy, 39
Establishing Focus, 13
Establishing Task Specificity, 30–31
Environment for Team Investigation, 16
Evaluation (Assessment)
  Expert, 67–68
  "For On-Paper-Research" Strategy, 59–60
  "Observing Leadership" Strategy, 24–25
  "Observing Team Activities" Strategy, 26
  "Of Real Objects" Strategy, 57–58
  Phase I, 51–52
  Phase II, 69–70
  Preliminary Team Assessment, 55–56
  Process, 51–52
  "Process Individual Assessment" Strategy, 53–54
  Product, 51–52
  "Quality of Research Project" Strategy, 75–77
  "Summative Individual" Strategy, 71–72
  Summative Process, 69–70
  Summative Product, 70
  "Summative Team" Strategy, 73–74
  Team Process and Leadership, 15
EVALUATION PHASE I, 51–52
  Rationale for, 51
EVALUATION PHASE II, 69–70
  Rationale for, 69

F

Flowchart on Cooperative Knowledge Production, 78
Forming Groups or Task Teams, 13

G

"General Procedure for Completion of Project" Strategy, 49–50
"Getting Acquainted" Strategy, 17
Groups or Task Teams, 13

I

IMPLEMENTATION PHASE I, 43–44
    Rationale for, 43
"Individual Intervention and Restructuring" Strategy, 64
Information (Data)
    Analyzing, 41–42
    Assessment of, 31–32
    Eclecting Processing of, 39
    Identifying, 29–30
    "Locating Information Sources" Strategy, 34–35
    "Organizing Relevant Data" Strategy, 40
    Prioritizing and Screening, 30
    Processing Phase, 29–32
    Training in Processing, 31
INFORMATION PROCESSING PHASE, 29–32
    Rationale for, 29
Initial Sessions, 12
"Interest Inventory and Ranking" Strategy, 21
Investigation and Knowledge Production, 7–8
    Flowchart for, 78

K

Knowledge Production (and Investigation), 7–8

L

Leadership, 13–14
    Assessing, 14
    Development of, 23
    Observing, 24–25
    Providing, 13–14
    "Locating Information Sources" Strategy, 34–35

M

Managing and Coordinating Tasks, 31
Materials, Securing, 44

O

"Observing Leadership" Strategy, 24–25
"Observing Team Activities," 26
ORGANIZATION PROCESS PHASE, 11–16
    Rationale for, 11–12
"Organizing Relevant Data" Strategy, 40

P

"Personal Inventories" Strategy, 18
Planning Research Projects, 15–16
Planning the Environment for Team Investigation, 16
"Preliminary Team Assessment" Strategy, 55–56
"Process Individual Assessment" Strategy, 53–54
Process Evaluation, 51–52
Product Evaluation, 52
Process Refinement and Implementation, 62–63
Product Refinement and Implementation, 64
"Project Decision-Making Procedure" Strategy, 45–46

Q

"Quality of Research Project" Strategy, 75–77

R

Rationale for Cooperative Team Investigation, 3–11
REFINEMENT AND IMPLEMENTATION PHASE II, 61–63
    Rationale, 69

S

"Scientific Inquiry" Strategy, 28
"Self-Assessment" Strategy, 27

"Summative Individual Assessment" Strategy, 71–72
Summative Process Evaluation, 69–70
Summative Product Evaluation, 70
"Summative Team Assessment" Strategy, 73–74

T

Task Teams, 13
Teacher/Instructor's Role, 9–10
"Team Intervention and Restructuring" Strategy, 65–66
"Time Management Procedure" Strategy, 47
Training in Information Processing, 31